Campus Schools

Campus Schools

New York City's Solution to Underperforming and Violent Schools

Mónica Ortiz

ROWMAN & LITTLEFIELD
Lanham • Boulder • New York • London

Published by Rowman & Littlefield
A wholly owned subsidiary of The Rowman & Littlefield Publishing Group, Inc.
4501 Forbes Boulevard, Suite 200, Lanham, Maryland 20706
www.rowman.com

Unit A, Whitacre Mews, 26–34 Stannary Street, London SE11 4AB, United Kingdom

Copyright © 2015 by Mónica Ortiz

All rights reserved. No part of this book may be reproduced in any form or by any electronic or mechanical means, including information storage and retrieval systems, without written permission from the publisher, except by a reviewer who may quote passages in a review.

British Library Cataloguing in Publication Information Available

Library of Congress Cataloging-in-Publication Data
Ortiz, Mónica.
Campus schools / Mónica Ortiz.
  pages cm
Includes bibliographical references
ISBN 978-1-4758-1525-2 (cloth : alk. paper) — ISBN 978-1-4758-1526-9 (pbk. : alk. paper) — ISBN 978-1-4758-1527-6 (electronic) 1. Educational change. I. Title
LA339.N5 O77 2015
371.209747/1   2015024400

∞™ The paper used in this publication meets the minimum requirements of American National Standard for Information Sciences—Permanence of Paper for Printed Library Materials, ANSI/NISO Z39.48-1992.

Printed in the United States of America

Contents

Acknowledgments	vii
Introduction	1
1 There Are No Quick Fixes	11
2 The Campus Schools	25
3 Collaborative Leadership: The Inner Workings of a Principals' Council	51
4 Under New Management: Campus Logistics and Operation	71
5 Where's the Boss? The Role of Central Administration	89
Conclusion: Creating a Better Transitioning Plan	103
References	111
About the Author	117

Acknowledgments

My deepest gratitude goes to the courageous principals in the Cuomo Educational Complex and the Marin Educational Complex and their staff, who graciously took time to share their experiences with me. In an era where accountability, autonomy, and empowerment converge to create a competitive and hostile environment for principals, these men and women stand out as true school leaders.

This book is about their stories.

Introduction

A safe and orderly environment conducive to teaching and learning is a key dimension of effective schools and a priority for educators. Creating a climate that is responsive to students' needs is instrumental to providing personalized instruction. School effects studies suggest that children who attend schools that run effectively increase their chances of success by 29 to 42 percentage points over those who are enrolled in less effective schools (Gottfredson, 2001).

However, this has been a difficult task for many large comprehensive urban schools that are restricted by space, resources, and overcrowding. Comprehensive schools in urban settings face a series of challenges: poor attendance, low academic achievement, and violence. The organization of large comprehensive schools, their structures, and policies can affect their potential to provide positive student support systems and their ability to control school violence and disorder.

SCHOOL VIOLENCE AND DISORDER

In attempting to respond to the problem of school violence and disorder, it is easy to forego school-specific aspect of violence. Identifying the factors that contribute to school violence and disorder requires an understanding of school environment and its impact on student behavior. Failure to do so increases the risk of instituting policies that discriminate, cause emotional distress, and do more damage than good, as is the case with zero-tolerance policies.

It is not always easy to distinguish between school- and nonschool-related factors. The boundaries between school and family, and school and the community, are often blurred. Poor urban and inner-city neighborhoods are characterized by high levels of poverty, higher crime rates, low level of home ownership, public housing, single-headed households, unemployment, and few possibilities of employment.

The instability or isolation of neighborhood organizations and institutions also undermine the social organization of the community. In addition, many of these neighborhoods lack collective efficacy, that is, community's shared values, norms, and goals. Children growing up in these neighborhoods experience an environment that is qualitatively different.

Schools that are located within the boundaries of these neighborhoods or serve students from these neighborhoods will experience a higher level of instability. The needs, realities, and experiences of these children are relevant to educators who are working with them in school settings and to the development of school safety and discipline policies.

Many attempts are made to cushion the effects of negative neighborhood pathologies, such as creating a climate where school violence is unlikely to occur rather than stopping school violence. This is achieved in a more personalized environment that reduces alienation, anonymity, and the impersonal character of many large schools. Many believe that this is a difficult task for large comprehensive schools to accomplish. As a result, the movement toward smaller schools has taken root.

SCHOOL SIZE

The movement toward smaller schools can be considered through two explanatory frameworks: social development of students and academic press (Lee & Ready, 2007). In general, research on the effects of small schools on school environment and achievement indicates the possibility for more learning by students, more personalized relationships, and increased student commitment. Although school size per se may not have a direct relationship with academic and social outcomes, it may be associated with some social benefits that may derive from a smaller environment, such as trust, commitment, positive teacher/student relationships, and a sense of belonging.

The sense of belonging cannot be understated when examining students' behaviors (Osterman, 2000). The experience of belongingness is linked to positive attitudes toward others and self. Students who experience a sense of belonging conduct themselves differently (positive attitudes toward learning, peers, and school staff; greater engagement; participation in extracurricular activities) and have a stronger sense of their academic and social competence.

The reverse holds true for students who feel rejected and alienated. Because they feel rejected, they are unlikely to try pro-social behaviors. The exclusion and estrangement from their peers is time and again associated with problems of behavior and linked with emotional distress, violence, and suicide. Attending a smaller learning environment may help develop positive relationships.

Small schools are frequently organized in a communal form with several characteristics such as shared values and norms, commitment to common goals, and shared decision making. These structures and processes are intended to create greater responsiveness to students' needs and wants with the expectation that they will experience greater commitment to school through increased participation.

Research also finds that support from teachers has the greatest impact on students' level of engagement and that schools contribute, over and above family and peers, to students' engagement or disengagement. If the quality of the interactions is positive and affirming then students' sense of belonging will be stronger. Responding to the need to provide students with opportunities for social development and academic press, educators have worked to design smaller learning environments.

Small schools are high on the list of recommendations. Smaller learning environments are organized in many ways, such as minischools, schools-within-schools, academies, magnet schools, and charters. Each of the organizational structures of the smaller learning environment has its pros and cons and may work better for some communities than others. In addition, providing students with school choice may increase student engagement since they are given more options for program selection.

EDUCATIONAL COMPLEX (CAMPUS)

As large urban school districts jumped into the small-school bandwagon, they soon realized that location of the new schools posed a problem. The design and implementation of campus schools was a creative solution to housing many small schools in a tight real estate and financial market. It also allowed for the use of school buildings that were readily available, although some modifications were required to accommodate the needs of multiple schools. However, that also meant closing the school occupying the building, which in most cases was seen as underperforming and violent.

For many districts, closing schools—a particularly disturbing trend in the last decade—has been the main tactic for eliminating underperforming schools and reducing violence. The strategy of closing schools, however, has many unintended consequences and it comes with no guarantees that establishing other schools in the same location will reduce violence and/or improve academic performance. It is still to be seen whether the new schools will pass the test of time and fare better than the original school.

As implemented, however, a campus is not a school, but rather a building that houses a number of schools, each one autonomous, with its own principal, educational commitments, and organizational practices. Campus schools can be thought of as subsystems within a system. While the small schools that comprise the campus schools have some features in common, the individual schools develop different patterns of norms and expectations, different school cultures, and different types of internal and external relationships.

Campus schools have unique characteristics that are not present in stand-alone small schools: large numbers of adolescents in one building; space sharing; and the possibility of being directly impacted by the educational and organizational practices of the schools within the building. In addition, campuses have a unique management system that relies on the collaboration of all the principals in the building.

There are three overarching problems of practice that are associated with the creation of campus schools: (1) the logistics of sharing space and resources; (2) the diverse organizational practices of the schools in the facility; and (3) shared expenses of campus management. The logistics of sharing space can be tedious and time consuming, requiring extensive collaboration among the principals. "Ownership" of the building becomes an issue. If a space is not assigned to a school then it belongs to no one, what is termed "un-owned spaces" or "shared spaces" (Osterman, 2000).

These spaces (i.e., gyms, cafeteria, auditorium) can become prime areas for misbehavior and the commission of violent acts because they belong to everyone and to no one. Schools located near these spaces are directly impacted by its use from the other schools. These interactions can be disruptive to the instructional practices of the schools located in the proximity of shared spaces. It can also create cultural conflicts among the schools since every school has its own culture.

The culture of the school is experienced through and reflected in its norms, values, and organizational practices. These practices encompass everything from teaching and learning to daily activities, including the articulation and implementation of a discipline code. Conflict may arise when the diverse cultures of the schools within the campus are not compatible with each other. Normally school cultures don't conflict with each other, however, on a campus the proximity of the schools within the building allows for direct exposure to other schools' cultures.

For example, in many secondary schools in New York City (NYC), wearing hats and do-rags is a great source of controversy because their use has often been identified with gang membership, and hats have been used to bring weapons into the school. However, educators' preferences in many small schools vary, and many allow their students to wear their do-rags and hats either because they perceive their use as cultural or because it imposes unnecessary dress restrictions on students.

This situation may cause conflict when some of the schools on the campus allow their students to wear hats and others do not. This situation may seem insignificant and inconsequential to the teaching and learning process, yet many hours are spent reconciling this difference. Other practices traditionally used in a large school to coordinate the movement of large populations of students (e.g., hall passes) conflict with the more relaxed environment of some small schools.

Another organizational practice that is an emblem of small schools is the reorganization of the traditional instructional day to allow for extended learning opportunities and personalized grouping. This also comes into conflict with other small schools that reside in a large building due to shared-space considerations. Creating these opportunities in a shared facility are challenges that the small schools' principals encounter every day.

COLLABORATIVE LEADERSHIP

The principals in a campus setting need to work collaboratively to ensure that all schools have the opportunities to implement their programs successfully. Collaborative leadership is a new concept for many principals. Unlike shared leadership in a school where the principal is still the authority figure, collaborative leadership requires the ability to build relationships, share control, and mediate and negotiate in good faith with others that have the same authority and autonomy as they do, namely, the other principals.

Collaborative leadership is a "sophisticated and mature style of leadership" and critical in campus management (Archer & Cameron, 2013). The principals, collectively, must decide how to best manage the campus so that it a safe and orderly environment. They must collectively agree on how to use their schools' funds and to equitably use the shared spaces in the building to reach their goals. For a school leader who has always had the final word on any decisions made being part of a collective is a unique position to be in.

The unique characteristics of campus schools create a set of challenges that are new to many principals and districts. What happens when norms and values are not shared across schools? How do these differences impact the campus and the schools within the campus? How do principals decide how much funds to allocate for campus management when they have their own schools to run? How is space use determined? Who decides what is equitable? What happens when principals don't agree?

There are no simple answers to these questions. In fact, there may be different answers for different campuses. Regardless of the answers, the solution lies among the principals. The experience and knowledge of the principals and their collective willingness and disposition to find equitable solutions to the challenges of campus management will determine what the right answer is. In the end it will be the principals that will make the difference in whether a campus is successful or not.

The creation of campuses may have seemed like the ideal solution to the complex problem of how to fix large, underperforming, and violent schools and provide smaller learning communities. However, the complexity and scale of their creation and the process by which they were implemented was underestimated and so was the context of the Impact Schools initiative status.

This is not to say that campus creation should be avoided—just the chaos that ensues as a result of a poor plan. Nevertheless, the campus success is a testament to principals' commitment to their school's success, even if at times their leadership was misguided. The Marin and Cuomo Educational Complexes is emblematic of the campuses developed during the Bloomberg/Klein era.

THE STORY OF TWO CAMPUSES

The chapters that follow depict the challenges, struggles, and successes of two campus schools in NYC. It is important to remember the context of the campus formation when reading their stories. The Impact status, the closing of the large school, the successful creation of small schools, and public scrutiny were just a few of the many challenges and pressures that the principals contended with on a daily basis.

Chapter 1 provides the historical context of the formation of campus schools in light of Mayor Michael Bloomberg's political agenda and his use of the Impact Schools initiative to close many of the large, underperforming, and violent schools in order to establish the new small schools. The Impact Schools initiative was a zero-tolerance approach to school violence and disorder. It included large deployment of law-enforcement personnel, installation of security equipment, and removal of students with high incidents of violence.

Once the school was declared "safe" it was then phased out. The phase-out process took four years, four years of mixed emotions. The process was intense and fraught with animosity from the members of the closing-school community; and at the same time the small schools' founders were excitedly seeing their vision come to life.

Chapter 2 introduces the new small schools in their prospective campuses, details their formation, their educational philosophies and commitments, and delves deeper into the impact these factors had on campus development. The Cuomo Educational Complex (campus) has six schools residing in the building; three of them are included in this book. This campus has experienced the greatest amount of school leadership changes. Some of the small schools have had multiple principals since their inception. Despite changes in the leadership of some of the schools, this campus seems to have a more cohesive campus management than Marin.

The Marin Educational Complex has five schools residing in the building; four of them are included in this book. This campus has experienced some developmental difficulties, not because of leadership turnover, but rather because of the collective nature—or lack thereof—of the principals.

The new campus structure created a form of school management—the Principals' Council—that was relatively new in the district, and nationwide for that matter, and had little research to support its development. Chapter 2 includes a significant number of quotes because it's important to "hear" the voices of the principals and staff members as they faced the challenges of campus development and management.

Chapters 1 and 2 read differently than the remaining chapters however, they provide an invaluable context to campus development and many of the concepts discussed in this book. Although you can certainly read ahead you may find it difficult to understand the rationale for some of the decisions made during this process.

Chapter 3 explores the concept of collaborative leadership in the context of the Principals' Council in the campuses. All principals have, at the most basic and elementary level, the same aspirations for their students: academic success and social growth. It is, however, at the implementation level that they may differ. These signatures go beyond their personalities; they speak of experience and knowledge.

Experienced principals understand the need for collaboration. In fact, they're constantly challenged on how to create a shared and collaborative leadership within their schools; they desire a community with shared norms and values. However, in a Principals' Council, this same concept takes on a whole different meaning for some principals. Whereas some principals will struggle with finding balance *between* autonomy and collaboration, others will choose autonomy *over* collaboration, regardless of the cost to the campus.

An in-depth look into the workings of the Principals' Council and its legitimacy among the principals will be discussed in this chapter. The principals discuss the challenge and frustration of working with colleagues that do not share or value the collaborative effort needed to make the campus work. They also reflect on what skill sets the campus principals should possess.

In chapter 4 the new management system on both campuses is explored. Although the new small schools were autonomous, they still had to manage shared spaces, shared expenses, and school safety. All of these issues were usually handled by the large-school principal, even during most of the phase-out period. Most new small-school principals had very little understanding of the logistics of running a large school.

However, as the large school became smaller and the small schools increased their register, it became apparent to the principals that they had to be an active participant in the management of the building. A campus management called the Principals' Council or the Principals' Leadership Council (PLC) was created to provide the principals with a forum for making decisions that impacted the building.

Chapter 5 looks at the role that central administration played in the formation and development of the Principals' Council and the campus. The critical role that central administration should have played was hampered by other events. In addition to the closing of large schools and the creation of small schools, central administration was also going through multiple restructurings that impacted the way schools operated and interacted with the administration.

The simultaneous efforts created a tumultuous environment for the small schools' creation and in many ways hindered the council development. Without training, support, and guidance, the council was left to figure out campus management on their own. This chapter also explores the role that district offices should have in the formation and development of campuses.

The conclusion provides a summary of findings and recommendations for both research and practice relevant to campus schools, their formation, the design of the new schools, and their management. Clarity regarding the campus experience provides district administrators, school leaders, and policy makers with a better understanding of the issues that impact the campus.

For school leaders, understanding the relationship among the schools and their impact on campus environment may provide the rationale and incentive to work collaboratively in creating a safe and orderly environment conducive to teaching and learning. For district leaders, understanding the turmoil experienced by the constituents of a closing school, while simultaneously establishing small schools in the same building, may provide the rationale for a more sensitive and planned transition that will consider the strong emotions involved in the process.

In the end, creating a campus school in order to provide choices for smaller learning environments to improve students' academic success in safe settings is complex and should not be understated. It is not about whether campuses should or shouldn't be created. This book is not about starting up new small schools or closing large underperforming schools. It is not about school size either. Nor does it advocate or oppose any particular reform.

This book is about the process of transitioning the large school to a campus of small schools and the impact on the staff and students, specifically on the principals charged with the task of transforming the climate and culture of a failing and violent school. And at the same time, this book explores the challenges these principals had to contend with in their own school while learning to collaboratively manage a campus.

The concept of collaborative leadership was certainly new to many. The assumption that principals would know how to collaborate, cooperate, and reach consensus was flawed, has had negative consequences, and has revealed missed opportunities. It stymied innovation and creativity in resource allocation and utilization. For new principals, becoming an effective school leader has a steep learning curve. However, being a new principal in a campus complicates that process.

It is the job of central administration to train principals to assume and embrace the collaborative leadership role that campuses need. Ultimately, the safe and orderly campus schools will depend on the collective effort of its trained principals.

Chapter 1

There Are No Quick Fixes

Although there are no quick fixes for academic underperformance and disruptions in schools, it doesn't seem to stop many policy makers from attempting to find them. Nor does it dissuade politician from focusing on these "quick fixes" when underperforming and disruptive schools become a perceived public problem. However, in attempting to respond to the problem of academic underperformance and school violence, it is easy to forego school-specific aspects and community context to seek explanations and solutions, which at times can create policies that do more harm than good.

Unfortunately, many of these policies seem to impact more overtly large urban school districts where the problems of violence and academic underperformance in public schools are more pronounced and chronic. This was the case in NYC where the public had had enough of school violence and academic failure and elected a mayor who promised to fix the problem. The public wanted—no, expected—the problem to be solved.

The solution was as complex as the problem. It would be easy to simplify the problem and say, "Let's just close the large schools and place small ones in them." The issue of violence and disorder had to be addressed first. It would be counterproductive to create new schools and place them in a building perceived to be unsafe. Parents would not want to send their child to a school that is not safe, regardless of the "smaller and personalized learning environment." Location did matter.

And then there was the issue of closing the large school. However, closing a school is not as easy as it sounds, regardless of the fact that it is underperforming and disorderly. There were students and staff concerns that needed to be addressed, inventory and equipment that needed to be accounted for, and records that needed to be safeguarded. In addition, the buildings needed to be retrofitted to accommodate the needs of the small schools that would be placed in the large school. It was a monumental task.

Undeterred, the Bloomberg/Klein administration took on the challenge of changing the landscape of schools in NYC. This transformation process included closing large schools and establishing new small schools, but first the mayor had to gain control of the schools. Bloomberg succeeded in doing so after an exhaustive campaign, becoming the first mayor since 1969 to be granted control over a divisive and underperforming school system of over 1.1 million students.

Once he was granted control of the school district, Mayor Bloomberg set out to address the issue of school violence. The mayor was swift and decisive in implementing his plan, holding both the New York City Department of Education (NYCDOE) and the New York Police Department (NYPD) accountable for the results. As new school concepts were sorted, vetted, and approved, the administration rolled out the Impact Schools initiative to address the issue of school violence and disorder.

IMPACT SCHOOLS INITIATIVE

In December 2003, Mayor Bloomberg announced a major safety plan addressing violence and disorder in some of the city's schools:

> Every student has the right to seek an education in an atmosphere free of fear or intimidation. The plan we are announcing today will turn around the schools most plagued by disruptive students and criminal behavior. It will identify problem students and send the message that disorder will not be tolerated. Whether a student chronically misbehaves or commits a serious crime, they will be dealt with swiftly, appropriately and removed from the school when necessary. (New York City Department of Education, 2003)

The strategy, Impact Schools initiative, based on the NYPD's Operation Impact, sought to identify schools with high numbers of incidents of crime, disorder, and unsafe conditions. Schools identified as such were declared Impact Schools:

> The Impact Schools were selected through an evaluation of data from both the NYPD and DOE. Schools with serious crime levels were identified by examining total number of incidents, incidents involving assaults (felonies and misdemeanors), incidents involving weapons or dangerous instruments and total number of major crimes. . . . NYPD data helped identify schools with emerging problems in the current school year. Troubled schools were also identified through a review of data on safety-related transfers, superintendent suspensions,

attendance and supervisory visits along with input from regional directors, regional superintendents and senior administrators. The list of Impact Schools was reviewed by the Department of Education, the NYPD's School Safety Division, the United Federation of Teachers (UFT) and the Council of Supervisors and Administrators (CSA). (New York City Department of Education, 2003)

The goals of the Impact Schools initiative were to establish a climate of safety by intensifying enforcement of the Discipline Code and correcting conditions at the schools that were conducive to disorder. The plan included: targeted deployment of police officers and School Safety Agents (SSAs); enhanced scanning and other security equipment; immediate removal and transfer of students with histories of disruptive behaviors; and training and support for principals.

On January 6, 2004, the mayor announced the first twelve schools in the city to be declared Impact Schools: ten high schools and two middle schools, mostly in Brooklyn and the Bronx. These schools were said to average six times more assaults and seven times more incidents with weapons than other city schools. As part of the Impact strategy these schools would receive double the amount of previously assigned SSAs and up to a dozen armed police officers from a new task force.

The schools were under intense scrutiny and were subjected to frequent walk-throughs by a task force consisting of NYCDOE and NYPD personnel. The task force, along with school administrators, would walk through the school with a ten- to fifteen-page checklist that included classroom instruction, condition of the facilities, cafeteria conditions and menu, student supervision, guidance, and even the condition of the bulletin boards in the hallways. Any items that were checked as needing improvement required a plan of action with a timeline for completion.

As intense, and maybe extreme, as these walk-throughs were, it was the first time many of the schools had received so much attention from central administration. Repairs were made to buildings. The halls and classrooms were painted. Bathrooms were fixed, painted, and even stocked. The hallways and stairways were cleared after the late bell, reducing student loitering and hence the possibility of fights. It was a comprehensive approach to reducing school violence by targeting school-related factors that created the condition and the possibility for disorder.

CONTROLLING STUDENT BEHAVIOR

Much of the focus of the Impact initiative was on controlling student behavior. Passes and logs were used to monitor student movement. Unauthorized movement could be the cause for detention, parental conference, or even suspension if the interactions between students and agents became hostile. The large number of SSAs and the task force created a tense situation on a daily basis. Many SSAs were insensitive to students' conditions, intolerant of any perceived misbehavior, and aggressive toward insubordinate students.

The relationship between the SSAs and the school administrator was tenuous at best. There was an ongoing power struggle over who was in charge at the school. This fragile relationship stemmed from the changing role of the SSAs under the NYPD and the authority of the principal. Although the changes, resulting from an investigation, occurred during Mayor Giuliani's administration, they became more intensely manifested during the Impact years. Mayor Giuliani appointed a commission to investigate safety in schools, which was under the jurisdiction of the Board of Education's Division of School Safety.

In 1996 the commission concluded that the Division of School Safety of the New York City Board of Education (now defunct) was poorly managed and was unable to effectively maintain safety in the schools and recommended that NYPD take a greater role in ensuring security in the schools (Murkherjee, 2007). Two years later, the New York City Board of Education voted to transfer control of security in the city's public schools to NYPD. The SSAs would be responsible for security at entrances, exits, and hallways; operating security technology; and having the power to arrest.

With SSAs now under the supervision of the NYPD, there were reservations as to who was in charge of discipline in the school—the principal or NYPD—a situation that became more contentious under Mayor Bloomberg's Impact Schools initiative. Whereas the SSAs were previously considered resource officers to the schools by the principals, working collaboratively to address student behavior, they were now seen as police officers ready to make an arrest. And since the SSAs were no longer under the jurisdiction of the NYCDOE, the principals had very little to say in their supervision.

Undeterred by the conflict, and with Mayor Bloomberg's focus on violent schools, a 150-member NYPD special task force was created in 2004 for the Impact Schools initiative. In 2005 an additional fifty task force officers were hired, bringing the number of agents to over forty-six hundred, along with two hundred police officers (Drum Major Institute, 2005; Murkherjee, 2007). Two months after the new initiative was implemented and additional agents and officers were hired, the mayor's office announced that crime had fallen nearly 9 percent.

However, with the mayor's zero-tolerance approach to school disruptions, the number of noncriminal incidents skyrocketed to an astronomical 72 percent since the initiative began in January 2004 (Gootman, 2004). The rise in noncriminal offenses was due to the criminalization of minor incidents. The officers and agents were issuing summonses for disorderly conduct, harassment, and noncriminal infractions, acts or misconduct that would have gone unnoticed at one time or been left to school administrators to handle.

The administration was sending a clear message to students that there would be zero tolerance for misbehaviors. Unfortunately, the increase in summonses and arrests correlated directly with an increase in student suspensions, a fact that was never reported or touted like the decrease in violence. Where do you put all the students that were being suspended? These students were still entitled to an education. What happens to all the students after suspension? They need to be returned to an educational setting. These questions had to be addressed if they were to call the initiative a success.

During the enforcement of the Impact initiative, low-offending students were placed back in their schools. High offenders, however, could not be placed in the same schools they were suspended from. These students would more than likely continue the same pattern of disruption. A resulting cyclical pattern of offending, suspension, and reinstatement would occur, with each cycle increasing the number of incidents.

To address the problem of reinstatement, programs had to be created to work with this high-risk population. Two new programs, New Beginnings and the Twilight Program, were implemented to serve students with a history of recidivism. To say that neither one exists today in the NYCDOE is a testament to the transient purpose of the programs, although both programs have been successful in other school districts because of their youth development approaches and supportive learning environment for high-risk offenders.

And had they been implemented earlier in NYC, they may have alleviated some of the problems in the large schools with high degrees of violence. Nevertheless, the programs served their purpose: remove serious offenders from the schools and provide them with an alternative educational setting, decreasing the number of violent incidents, and declaring the schools "safe."

It was important for Mayor Bloomberg to show that he could bring order back to schools. It was important that the parents believed that these school buildings were safe. The establishment of the small school depended on the creation of a safe environment. By June 2005, eighteen months after the initiative started, Mayor Bloomberg declared a dramatic drop in crime and disorder in the Impact Schools with some schools reporting more than a 50 percent drop in crime and a 57 percent drop in violent crimes (Herszenhorn, 2005).

Six of the original twelve schools declared Impact Schools were removed from the list. The initiative was considered successful on many accounts and soon other schools were added to the list. For those schools with a significant decrease in misconduct it was the perfect time to start phasing in the new small schools.

SMALL SCHOOLS IN NYC

In NYC, as with most large urban school districts, establishing "new small schools" was the major focus of school improvement. Like large urban districts, NYC embraced the small-school movement wholeheartedly with the hopes of increasing academic success and reducing violence generally associated with large-school settings. With the influx of funding from large nonprofit organizations such as the Carnegie, Annenberg, and the Bill and Melinda Gates Foundations, many small schools have been created to replace larger schools seen as underperforming and disruptive.

Although the small school is not a new concept in the NYC school district, it was usually reserved for creating alternative educational settings. For the most part, small schools were referred to as "alternative" schools and were created with the purpose of supporting students that were unable to succeed in a traditional school setting for a myriad reasons such as behavioral issues, learning disabilities, poor academic performance, child care, and poor attendance.

Many of these problems stemmed from dysfunctional families and/or problems associated with poverty coupled with poorly performing schools. Other small schools were created to meet the needs of specific student populations, such as immigrant students, many of whom came with interrupted or very little formal education. And others were established as innovative hubs for specialized programs such as the performing arts or career/technical education. Small schools provided families with choice.

Small schools have also served as the cradle for reforms in leadership, curriculum, and structures that have impacted the schools. The small schools allow for innovative practices to germinate and grow mainly because of their size, scale, and certain autonomy that is granted. It also allows for controlled growth and evaluation. This is an important component for any new program or initiative. In addition, it allows for greater input from multiple constituents.

In the 1980s there were about a hundred small alternative schools in the city. That number grew to over 425 by the 1990s. By the end of Mayor Michael Bloomberg's third term there were over 650 small schools in NYC, providing families the educational choice of a smaller learning environment. The increase in small schools was intentional and planned. It was the cornerstone of the mayor's political platform and part of his ambitious agenda to transform NYC's public school system.

SCHOOL CLOSURES

In the early years of the Bloomberg/Klein administration, school closings were shrouded in secrecy. Very little notice of the impending closure was given to school administrators, teachers, and parents. Sometimes the staff and parents found out via the media. In most cases the principal was usually informed a few days in advance. Unfortunately, the information was given to the staff in an emergency meeting.

An entourage of "suits"—central administration personnel, the superintendent, and union personnel—would come in to the building and meet with administrators, teachers, and parents. And as a group they would deliver the message of "doom" to everyone. It was not about having a conversation with the staff and students, nor was it open for discussion. It was then left to the principal to pick up the pieces of a shattered and battered staff, many of whom had believed that once the school was under control they could focus on instruction.

It wasn't until 2009—seven years after the first round of school closings—that activists became more vocal about the lack of transparency in the process (Arinde, 2009). They argued that delayed information and misinformation led to public confusion and panic about the status of their children's school. They also contended that the actions taken by the mayor were disruptive to the families and their communities, and that their impact on the students was long lasting.

More importantly, they maintained that these decisions were made without input from the people that were most impacted: students, parents, and local elected community officials. As a result of the backlash, a forty-five-day review period would be announced on any proposed school closing and a public hearing would be held at the school where the proposed closure would take place, at which time the Panel for Educational Policy would vote on the proposal.

The Panel for Educational Policy was the successor to the New York City Board of Education and was created to increase parent and community participation in decisions that impacted schools. However, many parents and local activists complained that this was a farce. The panel consisted of thirteen members, of whom eight were appointed by the mayor and could be removed at his behest, ensuring the mayor would get his way. Therefore, the fate of the schools was guaranteed regardless of protests from parents, students, and community members (Hannington, 2013; Otterman & Medina, 2010).

During the first term, much of the focus of Mayor Bloomberg and the DOE's reform effort was at the secondary school level, where urgent need for improvement was identified, but more importantly, it was the shortest and quickest way to improve graduation numbers and show academic progress. And since the Impact Schools were in such poor condition, anything done at this stage would have been an improvement.

A study comparing the original set of Impact Schools and nonimpact schools was conducted where school environment indicators such as demographics and academics were analyzed. The results of the study indicated that the large Impact Schools "were among the neediest in the city." Most of these schools had high student enrollment and seven of the original twelve were overcrowded and operating at overcapacity.

The Impact Schools experienced high teacher and student mobility; high academic needs as evidenced by students reading below grade level; racial isolation, with large populations of black students; poor attendance; high teacher-student ratios; low student expenditures; and high student suspensions and police incidents (Brady, Balmer & Phenix, 2007).

The Drum Major Institute for Public Policy, a nonpartisan and nonprofit organization, also released a study in 2005 on the conditions of the Impact Schools (Drum Major Institute, 2005). According to the study, the average capacity of Impact Schools was at 111 percent, with a couple operating at 180 percent capacity (i.e., 4.8 percent more crowded than the average city high schools). There were more overage students for their grade and a high population of blacks and poor students. In addition, the average per-student spending was $1,265 less than the per-student spending at schools similar to the Impact Schools.

The Impact Schools were large, underperforming, and disorderly, and had high incidents of violence. These schools also suffered from physical neglect and decay and from a multitude of problems symptomatic of years of neglect: high truancy, low graduation rates, and violence. And with less spending per student, there were fewer books and less furniture, equipment, and support services for students.

Unfortunately, many believed that the schools were just "too big and impersonal." Students were unknown by teachers and staff. The anonymity was surely the cause for the disorderly conduct from disengaged students. The only solution was to close the large schools and create small schools that would provide a more personalized learning environment.

And in September 2004, six months after the implementation of the new safety plan, the mayor and the chancellor announced the opening of ninety-one new schools; fifty-three of them were high schools. These schools were to be placed in underutilized buildings and in buildings where space was recaptured by removing administrative and program offices. However, much of the recaptured space came from the Impact Schools that were being closed.

LOGISTICS AND IMPACT OF SCHOOL CLOSINGS

The logistics of closing a school and its impact on staff and students cannot be understated. Many of the city's large-school buildings date back from early to mid-1900s. Records dating back to the 1920s and all the way through the 1960s were not digitally archived. This presented a space and custodial problem. The storage of a huge amount—thousands and thousands—of records required a significant amount of space. It also required a gatekeeper to safeguard and maintain their integrity.

The loss of these records would be devastating to the alumni since a duplicate copy did not exist. Therefore one of the new small schools would have to be designated as keeper of the records. They would also be responsible for sending out copies of transcripts to the alumni of the closed school. In addition, the designated small school would also be responsible for other records that needed to be safeguarded, such as employee records, payroll, attendance, and state Regents Exams. Since central administration would not store these records offsite they had to remain in the building.

There were other operational tasks that the principal of the closing school had to undertake. The school's inventories, furniture, equipment, and books had to be disposed of or distributed among other schools. Outstanding balances needed to be paid. Bank accounts had to be closed. As daunting as the task of handling the operational aspects of closing the school was to the principal, the human aspect was traumatic.

Strong human emotions—anger, bitterness, hostility, and defeat—were palpable. The staff and administration had just been branded and they felt demoralized. It was difficult for them to remain committed to the school. As a result, the school experienced a mass exodus of teachers, administrators, and staff, causing major disruption to the instructional process.

Those that remained to the end were sentenced to the Absence Teacher Reserve (ATR) or substitute-teacher pool where many languished for years since many of the new small-school principals did not want to hire a teacher from a school that had closed. For many of the new small-school principals, if a teacher had stayed until the school closed it was because they were unable to get another job and therefore "perceived" to be ineffective.

It wasn't any easier for the closing-school principal. If the principal did not abandon ship before the school closed he/she would be sentenced to closing one school after another. A closing-school principal was not expected to improve graduation rates or increase state exams (Regents) scores and therefore neither was improving instructional practices.

Consequently, the principal could not prove that he/she was an effective school leader regardless of the work that was done to successfully account for all students and logistical operation of the closing. As a result, the closing principal was unfortunately sentenced to closing one school after another. The stigma associated with being part of a closing school was long lasting and detrimental to the principal's career.

Students' experience during the phase-out period was very poignant especially at the high school level and for the last two remaining cohorts. For the most part, students were treated as second-class citizens. They sat in classrooms with old and defaced desks, working with outdated and tattered books, and learning in outdated labs while they observed their counterparts with the latest technology, new science labs, new books and supplies.

They were now considered trespassers where they once walked freely; hallways and stairwells near the small schools were strictly off limits. They could not mingle with the students of the small schools because they belonged to "the violent, disorderly, and failing school" that was being closed. Even entry to the building was segregated on many of the campuses; the new small-school students entered through one door and the closing-school students entered through another. The message was clear: Avoid cross-contamination of cultures.

Accounting for all students was another major concern for closing schools. The graduation rate for the schools ranged from 20 to 40 percent of each cohort. The remaining students needed to be placed or provided with opportunities to expedite the graduation process or encouraged to take the General Educational Development (GED). This was an extremely difficult task since many of the students remaining were overage, under-credited, and oftentimes had some learning disability. Other overage and under-credited students had behavioral issues and poor attendance.

No school would take these students voluntarily, especially with the increase in cohort accountability, nor did they want to contend with disciplinary issues that came along with them. The new small schools did not have to take them, mainly because they did not have the grade. However, even if they did have the grade, they would not take the students; the overage and under-credited ninth and tenth graders represented everything that went wrong with the large schools.

Not even the established small schools with a full complement of grades would receive these students and they didn't have to take them either. There was a "shield" around the small schools that protected them from these high-risk students. Nevertheless, with the closure of the school, these students needed to be placed. Unfortunately, they were usually placed in other large schools that oftentimes were also underperforming and disorderly.

Many of these schools were on the verge of being classified as underperforming and the conditions created by the increase in students from closing schools was sufficient to push the school over to Impact status. This created a domino effect of more school failure in order to implement more school-closure plans until all the large schools were closed.

The last graduation was especially difficult for the staff and students. The joy of graduation was tempered by the pending demise of their school. No more graduations. No more school dances. No teachers or administrators to visit after graduation. It was all gone. The remaining staff, with heavy hearts, would clear their rooms and offices, hand in their keys, and move on to uncertain futures.

CAMPUS SCHOOLS

The availability of facilities was among the greatest challenges that city school districts encountered as they moved to downsize large schools and create smaller ones. Building new schools is a costly endeavor. An alternative to building new schools is to retrofit large schools to accommodate multiple small schools, referred to as educational campuses, complexes, or multiplexes. A similar model of educational complex was created by the Coalition Campus Project in 1992 (Feldman, Lopez & Simon, 2006).

The project entailed closing two comprehensive high schools and establishing small schools within. This project was well developed, minimizing the impact on the closing school and the new small schools. And since it had the commitment and support of the parents and the community, it was a smoother transition for the schools.

The large Impact Schools were the perfect place to replicate campuses to house the new small schools. By 2013 an astronomical number of schools were closed—over 130 schools. Even some of the schools that were opened during the Bloomberg/Klein administration were closed. As a result there was a proliferation of over three hundred campuses created in the city. No other school district, large or small, had undertaken such a massive restructuring of a city's school landscape.

The Impact Schools that were closed went through a phase-out period. During this period, the large school would stop receiving incoming freshmen every year, effectively reducing its register. At the same time, the new small schools located in the large school would receive a freshman class every year, until they had a full complement of grades. This process usually took four years to complete.

However, the phase-out process was a chaotic one. "There is a heedlessness about the way this is being implemented," commented a parent advocacy group. Overcrowded hallways and disparities between the large school and the new small school created hazardous conditions conducive to jostling and fighting. There were clashes of cultures between the large school and the new smaller schools.

Throughout the phase-out process the retrofitting of the building continued. It was an exhaustive process with many stressful meetings. Creating the master plan for the campus was in itself a taxing and tedious process. Getting four, five, or six principals to agree on a plan was a strenuous exercise in collaboration and consensus building. Once a plan was agreed upon a construction plan was created to carve out the spaces for the new small schools while taking into consideration the needs of the closing school.

Every opportunity for construction was used for retrofitting the building: after school, extended holidays, winter and spring breaks, and the summer months. Summers were especially difficult since a large portion of the building was closed while summer school was in progress. At times it was necessary to relocate some or all of the schools for summer classes when central administration and the construction authority determined that the entire building needed to be closed. It was four years of relocations within the building and outside of the building to accommodate construction.

With the phaseout in full gear the principals worked on campus management. The Principals' Council, consisting of the principals in the building, was entrusted with the management of the building. They were responsible for safety and security, coordinating the use of shared spaces, and paying for shared expenses. Once the large school closed, the council would be responsible for the logistics of operating the building.

Central administration believed that assigning the operations to one of the small schools' principals would create the perception that he or she was the principal in charge. This would not only create conflict among the principals by potentially undermining their authority but also by giving the impression that one of the principals would have more authority and be in a potentially supervisory capacity.

A similar conflict was already being played out with the host- (closing) school principal. For the first couple of years, the host-school principal was responsible for the security of the building, ensuring that the safety plan was prepared; coordinating with School Safety, custodians, and cafeteria personnel; supervising and monitoring students' movements; and coordinating the use of shared spaces between the host school and the new smaller schools. The host school also paid for library services and all athletic programs.

And since the host-school principal was the point person for NYPD, NYFD, and PSAL, everyone recognized that person as the principal. The host-school principal was seen as the "building principal," something that the small-school principals did not appreciate. The conflict became more intense as the new small schools grew and the closing school got smaller. It eventually resolved itself when the host school finally closed. However, another conflict was brewing as the Principals' Council found themselves collectively responsible for managing a campus.

CONCLUSION

The Bloomberg/Klein area has been characterized by rapid change fueled by frantic and urgent need to alter the educational inertia and dysfunction of the current school system, creating in its wake much chaos and instability. Driven by national and state pressures for educational reforms, especially at the high school level, and the looming sunset of mayoral control of the school system, the NYCDOE believed that big changes were needed in a short period of time. They hoped for long-lasting effects but would settle for big impact.

However, without a true evaluative process, many of the reforms and restructuring were subjected to more reforms and restructuring while other emerging and evolving schemes and structures, such as the campus model and the Principals' Council management, were unsupported. Although there were a handful of campus schools in the city, they were not widely known or studied.

The Bloomberg/Klein administration left an indelible mark on an intractable educational system. And with the prodigious rate of school closing and opening they had in fact redesigned the entire city's school landscape in a relatively short period of time, albeit with many details left out of the picture. Nevertheless, the future of the new schools and the continuity of the established schools were dependent on not forgetting the conditions that created the schools long known as "dropout faucets" or failing to hold central administration "safe-harmless" on their role in creating those conditions.

Although economic and social conditions in the community added to the problem, it was the schools themselves that exacerbated the situation by creating conditions that promote social and academic upheaval. High teacher turnover, high student-teacher ratio, and high student mobility do not create opportunities for quality relationships that were being promoted by the small-school movement.

The quality of the relationships is critical for creating safe environments that are conducive to teaching and learning. Creating a humane learning environment requires that schools be provided with the necessary resources that create, promote, and enhance those teaching and learning opportunities. No one should be considered "safe-harmless" when these conditions exist.

Chapter 2

The Campus Schools

The reform's goal was to create multiple autonomous schools to replace large, underperforming, and disorderly schools. Creating smaller and more personalized learning environments was just one side of the coin in replacing the large schools. Providing greater options of small schools and choice in selection for families was the other side.

The diversity of school proposals was a reflection of the central administration's desire to provide a range of options for families. Each of the schools selected had a clear vision of their identity, focus, curriculum, instructional style, and school leadership. The principal and the small staff had high expectations for student achievement and engagement and a commitment to shared leadership with teachers, parents, and students.

The large building posed many challenges for the new small schools: space allocation in the midst of construction, agreeing on the use of shared space, a bell schedule that limited the use of shared space, and backlash from the closing school. And the Impact status only compounded the problems. There were still large numbers of SSAs and NYPD task force officers in the building. And there was still scanning to contend with on a daily basis.

The principals were hopeful and enthusiastic despite the challenges posed by the Impact status, the animosity of the closing-school community, and the perception of violence that the increased security created. Their greatest challenges came from making their vision come true in the midst of the chaos around them. The stories of the small schools on the campuses depicted in this chapter are in the context of the transition from large to small and the Impact status.

These are the lived experiences of people that cared and wanted to make a difference in students' lives. The principals and staff describe their educational commitment to create a safe and orderly environment and their effort to convince parents to send their child to their school on a campus that had a negative, disorderly, and at times violent history.

THE CUOMO CAMPUS

The Cuomo Campus, located in a major metropolitan city, is a huge four-story building dating back to the early 1900's. It served as a vocational and academic school to the local community. During the 1970s and through the 1980s it experienced high truancy and disorder. The school enjoyed a brief period of renaissance during the 1990s and was finally removed from the state's failing-school list, but this was short lived. Due to high truancy, increasing violence, and low graduation rates, the school was identified for closing.

In 2003 the mayor declared it to be a persistently underperforming and violent school. Under the mayor's directive, the large school, with over three thousand students, would phase out in four years and new smaller schools would reside in the building. By the time the old school phased out there were five schools with a combined register of approximately twenty-two hundred students on the campus.

A new school was added in 2007, increasing the campus population by a further 380 students, bringing it to a total of about twenty-six hundred students. A brief introduction to the participating schools situates a discussion of campus life on the Cuomo Campus.

Academy for MST Studies

The Academy for MST Studies is a six to twelve school established in 2004. It was one of the six schools slated to permanently reside in the large phaseout building. Its student population is approximately 60 percent Hispanic, 35 percent black, with the remainder a composite of other ethnic backgrounds. These percentages have been consistent since its inception.

The school has a "family-like" environment. Students enter the main office freely and are welcomed by the staff and the principal. The halls were bright, clean, and well decorated. Students were boisterous and yet very respectful. For the most part, students abided by the dress code of the school (black bottoms and white shirt).

Staff was pleasant and respectful to each other; they were also very young. Commenting on this fact the principal stated, "Two thirds of them have less than three years of experience." They adjust quickly to campus routines, for example, schedules for using the copy center or the library. According to the principal, "The experienced teachers . . . don't like the campus model." They demand a "teachers' café or a lounge." They have difficulty adjusting to scheduled times for campus shared spaces.

The principal, Mr. Messiah, who is calm and soft spoken, is the founder of the school, although he was not the writer of the proposal. The proposal for his school was so well received by central administration that two schools were created in opposite ends of the borough. He came to the school with previous administrative experience, having served as an assistant principal of supervision and as an assistant principal of administration at the high school level.

He was very involved in curriculum development when he was tapped to head the new school. His previous educational and administrative experiences made his school a good candidate to be located in the first floor of the building, a location that has some serious challenges and some great benefits. The school uses most of the first floor with the exception of the gym areas, which is shared space. The middle school resides in one wing and the high school resides in the other wing, commonly referred to as the east and west sides of the building.

The Academy for MST Studies is the only school on the campus to have a middle school. Although there had been conversations about changing the configuration, the school has decided that they like having both grade levels:

> We like both. We like the middle school and the high school. We don't like one over the other. One is easier to manage than the other one. One has more demands on you with state assessment, but both of them are something that we definitely want in this building, you know, for the community. (Mr. Messiah)

Convincing parents of middle school students that the building is safe is a different story. The building is still a scanning school. Many of the parents of incoming students were probably students at the large school or live in the community. "Well, part of it is the building itself, the reputation. Yes, you're a new name, but you're still old [Cuomo High School]," acknowledged the principal.

The school has been very strategic in its recruiting efforts, for example, meeting with the counselors of fifth graders; developing rigorous curricula; providing opportunities to earn high school credits through successful passing of New York State Regents Examinations; and mandating that students remain in their middle school until the ninth grade. Providing opportunity for parents to experience the school environment is an important component of their recruiting efforts:

> We have a couple of sessions that we run with the assistant principal, the guidance counselors, and myself. And we have it open, where they come in. We block out a time—nothing special; no special schedule. They'll come in and they'll see us in action. And sometimes they'll see some things they don't want to see—a fight, a discussion here or there—but most of the time it's very conducive to learning and very quiet. So they get a good impression.

Parents also get to experience the scanning process during orientations. They enter the building through the same entrance their child will come through in September, the main entrance. The main entrance is used exclusively for the middle school students, specifically the sixth graders, and for visitors during morning scanning. Parents have the opportunity to meet the SSAs assigned to scanning and the staff members assigned to the door.

Mr. Messiah encourages the SSAs to get to know the parents: "These parents are going to be here, so you might as well make a good relationship from the beginning so that when they come in, it's less of a hassle." He believes that the agents have been supportive of that goal. "You treat them great for two years, and then by the third year, they understand. We need to let go," the principal explained. The expectations are that by the third year, students (and their parents) should be able to handle the scanning process with minimal supervision.

When it comes to discipline, Mr. Messiah considers himself "a softie"; the teachers consider him "a softie." He believes that "once you get to the point of disciplining a child, it means that something along the way has broken down":

> I give people opportunities. I give people chances. You know, I think as humans, we all tend to have a bad day once in a while. And sometimes, I don't think children know how to deal with a bad day. So I'm a bit more compassionate about their behaviors. . . . I differentiate with the situation. I'm very non-tolerant at times of some things. Like I don't tolerate people cursing and yelling, and screaming, irate behavior, you know inappropriate behavior.

The principal thinks that his beliefs on discipline are not shared by most of his staff. "My teachers want strict—they did this; this is the consequence. Black and white, sequential." About 50 percent of the teachers will deal with their own discipline problems and are effective at deescalating a problem, and there are 10 percent "who care less," indicated the principal. "I was very hands-on at the very beginning and I think what I did was a disservice for my staff because I would be the one to give discipline."

As a result, many teachers expected him to come running when they called and address students' misbehaviors. He solved this problem by providing structured time for the teachers to address student problems and be more proactive. Mr. Messiah promotes a youth-development approach to discipline, teaching students to deal with issues and understanding why students behaved the way they did, what caused their actions and could they have been prevented.

Having a middle school has also made it particularly important for the principal to take a closer look at adolescent development and maturity. There are "silly incidents" like throwing paper that reflect immaturity. Other incidents reflect the sexual-maturation process of students creating competition and conflicts. The school has developed programs for girls, such as Girls Club, which provides a forum for conversation and discussion of issues affecting them. They plan to create one for boys soon.

The principal also believes that there are developmental behaviors that are specific to age and manifest themselves negatively in certain contexts:

> When we started our school, we had overage kids in the middle school. They were just—I mean maliciously—bad. Like they were looking for things to destroy, you know, like we had a brand-new set of furniture and by the end of the year, it was scarred. I mean, my desks, my tables, you know, everything was just—it got damaged. And there was a sense of frustration. They did not appreciate what we had. We realized that age-appropriate kids [for their grade] are totally different. Their behavior is totally different than the kids that we had. So, we experimented with some things with them. But very little [strategies] worked with that group until they got to high school. Once they got to high school, all of a sudden they feel like, "Uh, I fit here." You know, everyone around me is like me.

The school experimented with several configurations, such as mixing the eighth graders with the ninth graders for part of the day and separating the block schedules so that students did not have to sit in the same subject back-to-back. They had the same amount of subject class time; it just wasn't consecutive. Instructional practice was another area that the principal looked at when addressing student behavior. "They were just bored out of their mind," Mr. Messiah stated.

The lessons were not taught at students' cognitive levels; therefore, they engaged in disruptive behaviors. This also meant revisiting hiring practices. "I think we were willing to hire teachers who could relate to them and engage them in lessons." The school also developed its own handbook. "Because we are a six to twelve school, you know, we needed to explain to the parents exactly what it is that we expect your children to do."

The handbook articulates the expectations and consequences for violation of the school's discipline code, differentiating for middle and high school students, for the most part. Some infractions are treated the same regardless of grade, such as lateness, wearing hats and/or do-rags, or being out of dress code. The teachers created the handbook, however, the student council has the opportunity to tackle legitimate concerns. It gets modified to address students' needs, for example:

> Students were going for interviews—seniors. And they were not in dress code because of the shirt and tie. So some teachers, "Well, you're not in dress code." Well, you're beyond dress code, you know, in my opinion. But based on what

was written, you're not in dress code. So the student council made a big protest, saying, "You know what, there needs to be some differentiation in terms of our dress code?" So we put some things in place. We modified it to address their needs and their concerns.

The consequences for infractions ranged from detention to suspension. The school's suspension program is shared with the campus; instead of each school running a suspension program, which can be expensive, the schools on the campus pay the campus manager to run one program. The individual schools run the detention program. The school implemented a new Saturday detention for "cases that are not suspend-able but yet severe enough," explains Mr. Messiah.

He finds the Saturday program to be very effective for the lower grades, but it has been more challenging for the juniors and seniors since many of them work. Mr. Messiah speaks highly of the students and their ability to understand the concept of consequences. "Mr. Messiah, you need to suspend me," the principal says with a smile. "What I find with my kids is they'll take a punishment if the reason makes sense. If it's consistent and it's clear." The principal attributes his students' attitude to expectations that are clearly articulated in the discipline handbook and reinforced on a daily basis.

The head dean of the school shares this sentiment. Mr. Sargent, the dean, has been at the school for five years and has served as a dean for all five years. Unlike his principal, Mr. Sargent is neither "soft-spoken" nor a "softie." The dean, a tall, middle-aged man, states, "I take no prisoners." He explains his philosophy, "So my job as the dean, as far as I see it, is basically making sure the kids have an opportunity to come here, learn, and go home in the same shape they came, with a little more education."

He believes that this consistent enforcement of rules has been effective at preventing major incidents at the school:

> There are no riots. I have no gang issues. I have no knives. For the most part, there is no fighting. Nobody is getting hurt. My issues are silly issues, which is nice. Why? Because for five years I've laid down the law that says that this is not going to take place, not in the building and not coming in and out of the building. And they understand it. And they abide by it. And if you hold firm and as the new ones come in, they quickly learn from word of mouth of the existing kids that this is what you can do in the school and this is what the school offers you. And if you break the rules, expect to have a consequence.

Mr. Sargent's beliefs about discipline extend to the teachers as well. His expectation is that teachers should maintain an orderly and supportive workspace in their own classrooms.

You are considered expert enough to be paid for the job. You should be doing it as if you are getting paid for the job. I don't mind helping you out. I do mind you not having any ability to do so. It's just that I look at you and you are the professional in the room and you are allowing kids to run the space. Well, education can't take place if you can't control that room. If the room is out of control, they are not learning. It just doesn't work that way. You have to maintain some order.

Mr. Sargent, a social studies teacher, comes to the school with nine years of dean experience, having worked in the phased-out school before coming to this school. His experience at the phasing-out school was different since Cuomo High had approximately four thousand students. "There was an entire suite for deans.... There had to be, I think, somewhere between twenty and thirty deans." Students were alphabetically assigned to deans. Each dean was responsible for their caseload, regardless of whether or not they were the responding dean at an incident.

As senior staff at Campus One, Mr. Sargent had enough seniority to continue in the school until the year before it closed. This gave him time to observe the schools that came to the building, how they grew and operated. The main reason he decided to join this school versus the other small schools on the campus was because of eighth-period classes. He explains:

As I was leaving and walking down their one hallway, in their eighth-period classes, both the middle school kids and the high school kids were in their rooms working, writing, listening. And I walked through every day. It wasn't like once in a while; they did this every day as I was leaving.

He enjoys working with the principal. "My principal works hard to make sure these kids get an education," he explains. But he believes the principal is overly concerned about scores and how well students do on tests. "It's a political position," he states. Although he doesn't always agree or believe the principal is making the right decision, "I do respect him" because of "his concern for students and staff." The principal also allows him to do his job. "I have a wonderful principal.... There is no interference in terms of how I rein in the kids or do a superintendent's hearing or choose to do a principal suspension or however it gets set up."

The feelings of respect are mutual. Having a strong dean has allowed the principal to focus on school performance and developing stronger community ties to overcome the negative reputation of the old school.

College Preparatory High School

The College Preparatory High School was founded in 2007. It currently has an enrollment of approximately 370 students in grades nine to twelve and graduated its first cohort in 2011. The school was being housed on the campus until a permanent location could be found. In 2010 a decision to keep the school on the campus was made and it is now the sixth school to permanently reside on the Cuomo Campus.

The school is located on the fourth floor in one of the wings of the campus, its third move within the building. This section of the building is self-contained and is not shared with any other school. The hall is beautifully painted and decorated. The bulletin boards displayed student work. There is a "home-like" feel to the space—vases in the middle of the hall, potted plants by doors, student portraits, a mirror over the water fountain and even curtains in some rooms. Students—referred to as scholars—seemed happy to be there and in no hurry to leave although it was the end of the school day.

The signal for the end of the class period is music. "Some of our students have composed their own music. And that's what is played," explains Ms. DeGioulis, the principal. The scholars, in their uniforms, walked freely into the main office, even the principal's office, to make a call or sign up for laptop. The staff—referred to as professors—is young and inexperienced; most have less than three years of teaching experience. The professors appeared eager to work with the scholars and spoke warmly to them.

Ms. DeGioulis, a highly energetic woman with over twenty years of experience in the school system, is the founder of the school. She conveys a firm but motherly feel; the scholars respect her. She often referred to the students as children, a throwback to her years in middle school. Ms. DeGioulis also founded a similar college preparatory academy at the middle school level. She decided to open this school when her students were about to graduate from middle school and the parents requested a high school based on a similar model:

> I used to think that I loved middle school. I was very happy in middle school. And I didn't know that I would love high school as much. I would never go back to middle school or elementary school. High school is my thing.

The school's program requires that all students, not just the gifted and talented, be able to do high-caliber work. This poses a considerable challenge since the school does not screen its applicants and, therefore, receives its share of English Language Learners (ELL) and Special Education students:

> So we have the added responsibility of not just ensuring that the children pass the Regents but also making sure that we prepare them so that by the time they reach their junior year they are able to do [college-level] work, which means that they have to be on grade in terms of the reading and the writing. . . . It's given us the greatest fight. Because, with limited resources, having special-needs children, having ELL children, having children that are not reading at level, we have to service all their needs.

The principal and staff wear many hats in order to meet the needs of the scholars. The school has neither an assistant principal nor dean. "All we have to do is raise our hand and the kids are quiet. And that, you have to create, you know. You have to nourish." The school has its own lunch and physical education period. Having their own school space and dedicated cafeteria and gym periods for her school was important. "It was important to me, again, being very territorial, you know. I need to ensure that my children are safe. And I need to set the order."

To assist students in understanding appropriate behavior, the school uses a pledge as their standard code of conduct. The pledge uses a four-pillar approach to conduct: integrity, compassion, commitment, and communication. Every day, scholars recite the pledge. Ms. DeGioulis explained why it's important for students to embrace the pledge.

> I want the kids walking away with the understanding that they're here not because they want to get good grades, but they're here because their lives are transforming. They have the potential from this point on to become anyone they want to become. But what they become will really depend on the integrity that they have. If they're going to become true leaders, they must have these four pillars that will help them define success, not just a monetary or status label, but just inner success.

Violation of the school code of conduct is a demerit; each demerit references the pillar it dishonors. The teachers created the demerit system; students added behaviors they identified as demerits and which ones constituted merits. According to the principal, "It was working really well in the beginning, until the teachers began to abuse it and they started giving demerits out like they were going out of style."

The teachers who had poor classroom-management skills were quick to use the demerit system as a discipline mechanism. "It was just a part of a bigger problem that I eventually addressed. . . . Zero tolerance is only effective to a certain degree." Ms. DeGioulis believes that teenagers' behaviors are typical of adolescent development and that it is important to nurture students in order help them succeed. Otherwise, "You're just ensuring failure." However, she is not averse to dealing severely with a fight:

> We've never had any fights except for last week, where we had a major, major fight. And we had to deal with it. And I dealt with it very harshly. As a matter of fact, we have a superintendent's suspension coming up.

Unlike a principal's suspension, students can be removed, upon the principal's request, from their school and placed in an alternative site until a hearing is held. The principal is quick to clarify, "The discipline [problems] in our school—it's very low level." The lack of a SSA on the floor is evidence of the low number of incidents in the school. "We don't use them. So far, we've been very lucky. They're never here. They don't even appear for our lunch period." The school handles all problems that may occur.

Ms. DeGioulis refers to her school as a community of learners that includes both students and adults. She is very reflective of her practice and expects everyone in the school to do so also.

> And the understanding is that we are learners. And we need to get better at our craft, so that all the children can learn. And that means that we reflect a lot. We reflect a lot on what we do, on what's not working, on what should change, and how we can—how we can provide consistency toward children and remove some of the chaos. . . . We are trying to become more systematic with our practice. . . . Because, as we learned, we've had to make many changes here.

Ms. DeGioulis explains that the challenge of creating a community of learners involves constant conversations. Because the school is still growing, the principal meets frequently with the teachers and organizes staff retreats to touch upon some of the common beliefs. The continued conversations ensure that those common beliefs are reinforced. "Oftentimes just because a group of us knows it, does not necessarily mean that it's playing the same way in other people's minds," the principal explained.

THE MARIN CAMPUS

The Marin Campus is a large three-story building located in the same major metropolitan area as the Cuomo Campus. It serves a predominantly Hispanic population. Due to high truancy and violence, the mayor declared it to be a persistently underperforming and violent school and slated it to be closed. The school was to be phased out in four years with a completion date of 2008, when it would graduate its last class. When the school closed in 2008, there were five small schools residing in the building with a total population of approximately twenty-two hundred students.

The phase-in of the small schools occurred in stages. One of the schools, originally a program in the large school before it was declared underperforming and violent, became its first small school; two schools came in 2003; and the last two were established in 2005. The campus also has an evening program that serves older students in the city. This evening program is currently run by one of the principals on the campus.

The large school was still in existence by the time all five schools settled in. For the next three years, six schools—six principals—resided on the campus.

The campus has seen several leadership changes since the original principals began in 2003. Three of the five small schools have different principals.

Dual Language High School

The Dual Language High School was founded in 2005. It is a six to twelve school with a register of approximately six hundred students consisting of 100 percent ELL. All the students at the school are Latino; 85 percent of the student population is Dominican. The remaining 15 percent are of mixed Hispanic heritage. In 2009 the school admitted its first sixth-grade class. The decision to add a middle school was made in order to avoid a sixth school from coming onto the campus.

The school's space is beautifully painted and decorated. The environment is warm and welcoming. Students are dressed in uniforms. There is a banner that proudly proclaims its status as an A and "Well Developed" school (2008/09), referring to the two measures central administration uses to gauge school effectiveness. It has a staff of approximately fifty, two assistant principals, and two deans; 60 percent of the staff is Latino and/or Spanish speaking. The students and adults converse freely in Spanish and English.

The principal, Dr. Alvarado, is the founder and also the writer of the proposal for the school that would address the needs of the bilingual (Latino) and ELL population. She has a passion and a commitment to the ELL population's academic success. A Latina herself, she understands the challenges that the bilingual students have in meeting graduation requirements and adapting to a new country. She tries to foster a sense of community at the school: "There is a level of comfort that the students feel. . . . This feels more like home to them."

Dr. Alvarado explained that she had worked in two other schools that were considered "problematic" so she already "had an idea of what a challenging school, based on discipline, based on safety and security, looked like." Her concern was to "make sure that I had the best resources for my children." Her staff was just as receptive to the idea of coming into the building. The school's original location was on the third floor of the building. "We were in a corner where nobody was coming up to visit, where there was not a lot of traffic. It was a really good situation."

The school is now located on the first floor and part of the basement. It is the only school located on the first floor since the remaining space is considered shared campus space. The shared campus space includes the auditorium, campus manager's office, conference room, clinic, and other offices. In the lobby there is a semicircular reception desk where security sits and visitors sign in. There is also a scanning machine that students and visitors have to go through when they enter the building.

Dual Language is the only school on the first floor. The number of students moving through the space is limited to change-of-class periods and those entering the building. The school's location on the first floor seems to bring with it a greater sense of responsibility for the principal. Dr. Alvarado referred to herself as the "building principal." "If there is an incident that happens . . . that falls on me. . . . I'm in charge of safety and security with Mr. Gerente. Any building issues that come on my table, of course I solve it with the council, but at the end of the day my signature goes on it."

Although she does believe that removing scanning is an option for the campus, she frames it differently for parents:

> But I don't kind of frame it that way and just say, "We're here with your children, your babies." We're going to treat them as if they're our own, and we don't know things that may come into the building from adults, from children. And I know sometimes it's scary to hear, but I'd rather be safe than sorry.

Dr. Alvarado comes across as a tough, no-nonsense person in a quiet way. She takes great pride in the disciplined way her school is run. "Our school is very well managed, in terms of discipline. We have 100 percent uniform policy. The students, for the most part, abide by it." When asked about her approach to discipline, Dr. Alvarado explains:

> I believe in immediacy. I believe in nipping it in the bud as soon as possible before it escalates. I believe that not only I should know, but your parents should know, the community should know, the cook should know if you did something wrong. I feel like the more children, even though they may see it as we are nagging them and we can't give them space to breathe, the more they know that people care about them, the better that they will do. And they have to also understand that when they're disciplined, when we're showing you that this may not have been the right choice—because it's all about the decisions that you make.

Dr. Alvarado believes that her approach to discipline includes guidance and youth-development components. "There is always a conversation . . . but sometimes those conversations just become repetitive." Listening to students is important, "but also setting structures and procedures for students . . . they are human beings, and people need rules." These structures and boundaries have been instrumental in her school success: "Our students have a very good relationship with the adults, but they know certain boundaries not to cross."

The school has its own discipline policy created by the teachers and articulated in the "administrative handbook" that includes consequences for infractions, such as lateness or violations of school rules. Although teachers created the handbook, the students have the opportunity to voice their concerns on issues that affect them through the Supportive Learning Environment Group.

The group consists of students, a parent, and the coordinator of student activities (COSA). This group was not part of the original proposal of the school, but rather resulted from an articulated need of students to voice their concerns about school, home, transition to a new country, and their aspirations. The principal explained that students who are new to the country and are learning a new language often find themselves the victims of the ignorance of others, whether they are SSAs, cafeteria staff, or other adults.

"Other adults who don't know the language [Spanish] . . . often think that if they yell at the student, they'll understand better. So if I tell you to put your book bag in the machine the first time, and you didn't understand me, if I yell at you, you'll understand me the second time." For these and a variety of reasons, students want to be more involved in the community. "They wanted to do more community service, helping people, helping out in the school, helping outside of the school." As a result, the school has an extensive community service program funded by a Good Friend Community Grant.

Dr. Alvarado's no-nonsense approach extends to her relationship with SSAs. However, unlike her philosophy on discipline, she has a "no-tolerance policy" regarding School Safety. "The relationship has been very much strained between School Safety and myself. I found that a lot of agents wanted to just be people who berated kids . . . and others just wanted to be friends."

She has seen numerous activities that she characterized as inappropriate, such as cursing and conversations laced with sexual language. She attributes this behavior to several factors: lack of training and supervision, motivation, age (some agents are only a few years older than her students), and low salary. "I think that things have gotten better. I think that they are learning that they have no choice but to change, because we've been really on them about changing."

Ms. Rodriguez, the dean of the school, is also a tough-minded woman, with over twenty-seven years of experience with the city's educational system. Unlike her principal, Ms. Rodriguez's toughness is tempered with a sense of humor and a quick smile. She regularly switches languages when reinforcing a statement or using an adage to explain something. Her entire educational career has been at the Marin Campus. She started as a bilingual secretary and then became a Spanish teacher. After ten years of teaching, she became a dean.

She was also an assistant principal for a brief stint but after two years she decided to return to teaching and the dean's position. "That was not a good match and I like this; this was my strength." Ms. Rodriguez has been with Dual Language a year. She worked at another school on the campus while she was an assistant principal. When she decided to not continue with administration, Dr. Alvarado offered her a position as a dean. Ms. Rodriguez is one of two deans, both women. She works with the high school level, and the other dean focuses on the middle school level.

Ms. Rodriguez's belief about discipline, just like her principal's, is that appropriate behavior stems from strong enforcement of uniform compliance. When questioned whether the school had a discipline policy, Ms. Rodriguez stated, "I believe so because it is a uniform school. That is the first thing. This is a uniform—it is the only uniform school on the campus."

Deans go to classrooms and do spot checks on uniform adherence; students are given detention slips for noncompliance. The uniform policy is enforced through detention. Ms. Rodriguez believes that uniforms eliminate many of the problems associated with discipline:

> Because then everybody—they are all, not kind of—because they are all dressed the same, then there is no time for chatter about, "Oh, look at your new sneakers," or "Look at your new blouse." There is not a conversation around "I got the latest sneakers, the latest this." That is out. And so when I talk to them sometimes about the uniform, "Here is the thing. When you go to the interview are you going to show up like this with the pants hanging or are you going to show up like this? You know, that is in the world, in this real world. So how do we get them looking at the competition? You know, because it is about the look. And they are so, it's about the look. And I say, "When you walk into a room, what are they going to look at? *Calzoncillos* [underwear] on the back?

When it comes to staff enforcing this policy, Ms. Rodriguez stated, "Maybe half or more get it." Some teachers are focused on instruction and may not be active participants in this enforcement policy. "So there are occasions where it is not on the forefront of their minds, but I know that it is important to them as well." Although the disposition toward the enforcement of school policy is not consistent among all teachers, Ms. Rodriguez continues to support them in this endeavor.

The High School for Performing Arts

The High School for Performing Arts was founded in 2003. It is a nine to twelve school with approximately four hundred students. As a performing school, students are selected from a pool of candidates who audition for a seat. Unlike the other schools on the campus, the High School for Performing Arts did not start up at the Marin Campus building. It was moved from its start-up location in 2004 and slated to permanently reside on the third floor of the campus.

The hallways of the school, just like the others in the building, are beautifully painted and clean. The bulletin board displays students' work and school information. There is a large display case with trophies and awards the school and students have won. The staff was professional and pleasant when they spoke with me. The students seemed focused on whatever task they were engaged in and interacted in a respectful manner.

Dr. Cruz, founder and principal of the school, a known and still-performing artist, speaks passionately about the school and music. "I can talk about this all day." He was the writer of the proposal for the school, although that was not his intent.

> Although there's music in several of the schools in the [district], there was no high school of music that kids actually come to audition with that being the criteria and emulate some of the other schools that would offer the kids in the [district] the same kind of enrichment, the same kind of offerings of high-quality music.

When the call came out in 2000–2001 for educators to offer proposals to create small schools as part of the New Century schools, Dr. Cruz wanted to "join a team." However, he found that no one wanted to create a high school for music. There were proposals for performing arts but "they were putting too many things in the mix" he explained. He believed that focusing on too many areas, such as dance, theater, visual arts, and music would cause the small school to fail. "My idea is to have a strong science and math and English department, and then have a concentration in music."

Students who want to come to the High School for Performing Arts must audition. The school does not look at their grades but their ability to play an instrument. All students are required to be assessed by the state's music association. The assessment process requires the student to perform in front of a judge as a soloist and as part of an ensemble. The following year the student has to perform against their previous score and move one level up. "It's nerve-wracking," explained the principal. However, all students go through this process. "I think it gives our school credibility as a music school."

Dr. Cruz comes to the position with seven years of administrative experience and a doctorate in music education. He was an assistant principal in a large school, the school that incubated this small school. Although it was a large school, it was not slated to close like other high schools. Unlike the other large schools, it had very strong community support including a strong alumni organization that prevented the possibility of that school becoming a campus.

As a result, the High School for Performing Arts had to move. "This has nothing to do with you personally. We don't want you to leave," remembers the principal. Dr. Cruz understood the politics involved in the decision and the logistics. The move to the new location was difficult. For one thing the school was being moved to an Impact building. And secondly he was never part of the decision process.

He was not informed of his new location until late spring of 2004. Students had already auditioned and were informed of their acceptance to the school—at their original location. "They should have told us, so that I could have prepared my school community for the move, and to tell the incoming students where we are." Many parents took exception to the new location and did not want to send their children there. The large school had been declared underperforming and violent in 2004, a designation that led to its impending closure.

> I mean, the superintendent had told us, "They're looking for schools like yours to put in there, to turn that whole building around and the whole community." That's a lot to put on a new small school, sure.

Dr. Cruz had to do plenty of public relations to convince parents to allow their children to come to the location. He was quick to point out to parents and other constituents that his school was not disorderly and violent just because it was placed into a large school that was disorderly and violent: "In any event, a real difficult time for our school." On the other hand, he did not have to convince the teachers to move with him, "I didn't lose anybody. In fact, I had to grow." The staff he hired for the second year were all new and had not worked in the previous school.

The new teachers did not know of Marin Campus's reputation; neither did he. "I mean I knew there were issues. I don't want to say a problem place, but it was having its challenges though, and [it] had turned into an Impact building. . . . It's not like I really had a relationship with anyone in the building. I didn't know anybody, frankly."

Dr. Cruz tried to focus on the advantage of his current location, that is, its proximity to his community-based organizations (CBO) partner, the College, which is located near the Marin Campus. The College and the High School for Performing Arts have been partners since the proposal was written and have received much support from the college's president. The location near the College has allowed more students to participate in joint programs. The school has even been able to conduct classes there.

The school currently has two assistant principals: one for administration and one for supervision. The assistant principals and the teachers have been instrumental in creating a discipline-policy handbook that is given to the students every year. At the start of the school year, the principal reviews the discipline policy with the teachers; teachers review the policies with the students in their classrooms. The campus manager visits the classrooms to speak to students regarding the school's and the campus's expectations for behavior.

Dr. Cruz believes that youth development needs to be considered when enforcing the discipline code. "Everybody can make a mistake," he stated.

However, patterns of repeated misconduct or severe infractions will not be tolerated. Physical altercations automatically end with the student being suspended. Dr. Cruz is also emphatic on zero tolerance for the use of profanity:

> I don't take cursing in school. You know, kids curse like they're talking about anything. And I tell them, that's not allowed. You're responsible for what you do. You're responsible for what you say—and then especially if it's directed at someone. I don't mean that you're mumbling. I mean you actually, you know, pointed a finger and said something really grotesque to somebody or to an adult—zero tolerance. You're going to get suspended. There is no question about it. No arguing. . . . So, if it's the first time, and it's done in anger, there may be some flexibility there, depending on the circumstances. But they know that cursing is not allowed. And I have suspended just for cursing.

According to the principal, his staff is supportive although they may not share his belief about discipline. He is quick to acknowledge his staff's effort in getting the job done. "Staff works hard, they really do." He only has one dean, and teachers volunteer for hall and lunch duties. When talking about the students, he is reflective:

> They're not bad kids. But, I mean, I have my share of knuckleheads. I have Special Ed. I have challenging situations with kids. But they made the school through music. So I have that for them. And it's funny how some students who are problem kids in some classes are not problems at the college or in their ensemble. And I think it's because of the structure. If you play the trumpet, you know, you have a responsibility to be in your chair, to have your instrument ready. . . . And when they're disciplined enough in music, it segues into the other classes.

Dr. Cruz has high expectations for his students and his school. "What I want is that it's recognized as a high-standard, national-level performing high school."

The High School for International Studies

The High School for International Studies was established in 2005. It is a nine to twelve school with approximately 450 students. It is a 100 percent English as a Second Language (ESL) school. Although its biggest population is Hispanic, it has students representing over twelve countries. The school is located on the second floor and is one of the five schools slated to permanently reside at the Marin Campus.

The principal of the school, Mr. Lipchitz, a tall, lanky gentleman with a propensity for sarcasm, was also the concept-paper writer. He came to the school with no administrative experience and did not want an assistant principalship. "I would never be an AP because the AP is the one that questions the principal's vision. So if I'm not going to be the one with a vision, I don't mind being the teacher in the room. But I'm not going to push someone else's vision."

He is the only instructional supervisor. The school does not have any compensatory positions, that is, positions where a teacher is relieved of teaching duties to perform, in most cases, administrative tasks, such as program the school, coordinate testing, and carry out dean duties. Some of these administrative duties are paid for on an overtime basis, however other administrative positions do not exist such as the dean's position. Mr. Lipchitz is adamant about teachers teaching.

> I really believe that little thing I told you, when I was being sarcastic, that's what I tell the teachers. You don't hire an electrician and then reward them by saying, "If you're a really good electrician, pretty soon you won't have to do electrical work." If you have the best electrician you can find, you have them do electrical work. You don't say, "I'm rewarding you now, because I'm going to make you a dean. You're such a good electrician, you're going to be a dean. And you'll get some time off." Why would they want time off? That's what they chose to do for a living. So you take people that know their art, know their stuff, are the best teachers on the planet, and you reward them by taking them out of the classroom, give them a clerical job? Yeah—No. So yeah, the teachers teach.

The programming of the school is also unusual for a high school. Teachers have parallel programs. This makes changing a student's program somewhat easier; you can change one course without disturbing the rest of the program. This also means that teachers may have more or fewer teaching periods than the typical five teaching periods; however, the teachers agreed to this structure. The principal understood his inability to program the school with the restrictions set forth in the contract, room availability, and predetermined lunch and gym periods. He decided to give it to the teachers to resolve:

> "Great. Here it is. How many hours do you guys want? I'll pay you. Fix it. I can't do it. I accept my weakness." And they left and they came back three days later. And they said, "It's completely impossible to program the school with four classes and a fixed lunch. So we have to use . . ."—because they couldn't move the lunch—"but we've agreed to take four in a row one time a week each." Done. . . . After that, I never tried to program the school again. I asked for a committee. I gave it to them. I said, "Here are our limitations. Now we have six rooms. We have this lunch period. We have these gym periods." And they always made the exception to something in the contract.

The teachers are organized in teams—subject and grade levels. The grade-level teams meet on a daily basis; subject teams meet once a week and the whole staff meets once a week. Mr. Lipchitz acknowledges that between the parallel programming and lack of compensatory time, the school is an expensive model. "That's actually expensive," he explained. "So you can make more money in this school, but you can't get out of teaching if you're a teacher."

When it comes to discipline, the school's approach is also somewhat unusual. The school has no written discipline policy nor does it have a dean. The school does have a social worker and a guidance counselor. Discipline issues are dealt with in the teacher grade-level teams since they share the same students. Teacher teams have a leader; in most cases it is a senior teacher.

During their daily meetings, teams discuss students' behavior, among other issues. The senior teacher helps the team decide whether the behavior requires a call home, guidance intervention, or parent conference. "It should always be through the lens of what are we going to do to make this kid successful in school. You know, it's not a punishment thing," stated the principal. When parents are called, they meet with the team:

> There's never been one kid and one teacher. So they meet with the team, which is much more powerful for a parent to come in and say here are some of the things, here are some negative things, here are some ways of fixing it.

On the occasion that a student needs to be removed from the classroom, teachers can call someone for assistance. There is usually a school aide who monitors the hall and can escort a student to the social worker's office or to the principal's office. The expectation is that as a teacher you are responsible for managing your classroom. "So, this hasn't been a place for everyone to work. I know that, because some people have left. But it's the structure of the school," explained the principal.

Nevertheless, he believes that it helps teachers understand that there are no quick fixes to problems. "Things are not always just as cut and dried as they seem." Mr. Lipchitz believes that because of the collaborative nature of the school, teachers have to work together. "I can't tell them what I want and at the same time mandate and micromanage other stuff," explained the principal. "They work on it. And as long as we're getting results, it's okay."

School for Professional Careers

School for Professional Careers is the oldest school located on the Marin Campus. The school was originally a program in the phase-out school; it ran for over fifteen years. The school, a nine to twelve high school, was established in 2002 with grades nine and ten. The program became a school several years before the phaseout of the large school was announced. It currently enrolls approximately five hundred students, 61 percent of them girls. The school also has a large Hispanic population (62 percent), consistent with the other schools on the campus.

The proposal to convert the program to a school was written by the principal and an assistant principal of the large school. When the principal of the large school decided to retire the assistant principal then became the principal of the newly formed school. In 2009 the founding principal retired and the assistant principal, Mr. Girgenti, became the new principal. It was Mr. Girgenti's second year at the small school.

Mr. Girgenti's entire educational career has been on the Marin Campus, from teaching to administration. He has been in this building for over twenty years, although he won't specify. He did indicate he was in this building when renovations were made twenty years ago:

> I've been in that building my entire career, from a teacher to administrator, to teacher position, to assistant principal and now a principal in that building. So I'm the most senior person in that building. I've been there a long time. I don't want to tell you the number of years. . . . And I know that building like the back of my hand. I've been there when they modernized the building twenty years ago. So I know every nook and cranny in the space.

Mr. Girgenti was a math teacher, a dean, a programmer, an assistant principal of guidance, and an assistant principal of organization. Two years prior to the closing of the phase-out school he moved to Professional Careers as an assistant principal. He began the position of principal with strong analytical skills, a youth-development approach, and a sense of urgency:

> The program in the beginning was the honors kids of the phase-out school. It was the best students. So those kids are self-motivated. They are bright.

> So over the years—and I think it's the system that does it—the kids became mixed. Unless you can sustain that great reputation to attract great kids, you're going to start getting kids that don't want to be there, that are very weak; level-one, level-two students. And you're going to have to work a lot harder to get these kids to be successful. . . . My job is to get that turned around and start attracting kids that really want to go here.

The school was experiencing a downward trend in attendance and student progress, discipline was a problem, and instruction lacked focus. The previous principal had no assistant principal for many years, to help with administrative responsibilities and instructional support. The school needed structure and systems in key areas. Mr. Girgenti's priority, as an assistant principal, was to put systems in place for the guidance department.

There were very few systems in place here. First year was all guidance. Their records were a mess, student records missing, transcripts not updated. Every time they received an over-the-counter student, they never updated the transcript. So, that was a big job.

In addition to creating systems for recordkeeping, he provided the guidance staff with professional development in order to meet the needs of challenging students. Once principal, Mr. Girgenti rearranged the use of space, bringing the guidance counselors, attendance coordinator, and the dean all into one space. "I created a team." By placing everyone in one big administrative hub, the counselors and the dean and the attendance coordinator could collaborate and address students' needs. "So, that worked out well."

He also created a student handbook that included the school's discipline code and graduation requirements. He then proceeded to tackle instruction. He believed that teachers received little support or professional development under the previous administration and also received little supervision. "And there's not one teacher in the eight years the school has been in existence that ever received an unsatisfactory observation," indicated the principal. He explained his predecessor's philosophy about teachers:

> So she depended on teachers. And she believed in the power of teachers, she really did. And that's good. The only problem is they didn't have guidance and focus and any kind of supervision about standards, and teaching to the standards, and making sure their kids are succeeding on standardized exams. It's basically teachers got together and did what they needed to do, hopefully. Some did, some didn't, you know. They're all old school. They want you to leave them alone.

"I really have a lot of love for the teachers there," stated the principal. He believes, however, that teachers need support in order to be held accountable. He has reorganized the day so that 90 percent of the staff is available during students' lunch period and used it for professional development through Circular 6 (a menu of assignments agreed upon between the principal and the teachers' union).

Mr. Girgenti has a calm, Zen-like demeanor, very focused—qualities that came in handy when assuming responsibility for this school. Discipline and culture were big challenges. "I try to address the student culture here and the staff culture here, being very positive, and teaching teachers how to deal with students better." His approach has been two-pronged: creating structures and systems for student discipline and training teachers on how to deal with student behaviors.

Student cutting was a major issue: "Like kids would go to class whenever they wanted." He had to create a "very comprehensive plan" since he lacked the manpower, and he had to deal with the fact that he had rooms on the other side of the building. A two-color-coded pass system was created to differentiate whether the students were cutting—or late because they came from the other side of the building.

Another problem was students fighting. "I mean we had a lot of fighting in the school. But that stopped." Part of our plan was to have guidance counselors go into the classrooms and do role-playing skits with students and discuss different scenarios and communication techniques. "But the message got out there that we're not playing. So the kids went to class, you know. And it works. Now, is it perfect? Far from it."

His experience as a dean came in handy in this situation. "I worked with really difficult kids, tough kids. And I learned how to talk with kids." His approach with teachers was similar to the students, teaching them how to deal with students and understanding their role in modifying behavior. Creating awareness and sensitivity to students' lives was important.

He provided teachers with training. "Because 95 percent of the problems don't have to get to a level [of severity] if the teacher learns how to deal with students in a different way, a more respectful way, and shows compassion and caring," explained the principal. "Teachers' attitudes and the way they communicate with students will impact their desire to come to school. Teachers are sarcastic. And they think it's funny, but it not funny when it's at someone else's expense."

The principal's goal is for teachers to develop the skills necessary to work with the school's population in order for teaching and learning to happen. "I want to make them aware of the reasons why kids stop coming to school, that they're frustrated with school and they're not successful." He knows that it will take time, energy, and consistent reinforcement of the message. He recalls an incident that happened several days after a training session:

> What happens? A teacher within two days takes the kid's hat. You know what the kid did? Took the teacher's laptop. So I have them stand there with the hat and the laptop. I said, "Okay, we'll count to three; we're going to exchange." That's what I said. And they did, and they laughed. But it wasn't funny, because they got heated. And the teacher was angry. She figured, "I'm the teacher, I can do what I want." No, you can't touch kids. You can't do that.

"It's a constant battle," the principal said in his calm, Zen-like manner.

Mr. Espada, the dean, has a humorous perspective on school and campus life. He was a science teacher before becoming a full-time dean. He was also dean at the phase-out school for three years before coming to Professional Careers three years ago. When asked why he became a dean, Mr. Espada explained:

Well, it was something like this. It was an interview for you for being a dean. I didn't want to be a dean. I wanted to be a classroom teacher. They said, "Well, we are going to have to let you go then." And I said, "Okay. I will be a dean." And they gave me the radio. That's how I got to be a dean.

Of course, being a dean in a large school is different than in a small school, according to Mr. Espada:

The main dean in a large school sits in an office and the minions go out and they bring all these kids in. And you sit there and you make a decision about what you are going to do to them. Here you are the chief cook and bottle washer. You have to be out there. You have to have a presence. They have to know who you are. They have to know that you are fair. Whatever you do to them you have to do to somebody else. It is very different and it is active.

Mr. Espada explains that his role is like Dr. Jekyll and Mr. Hyde. He'll do whatever it takes to get them to class on time: "Scream, rant and rave." But when he works with students one-on-one he functions as a counselor. Many teachers are not aware of students' home situations and its impact on behavior. He works with the counselors to help students develop skills to address or cope with their problems. He finds that teachers don't always want resolution, but punishment:

You know, skin them alive and filet them and kill them in front of the teachers so you can see that you've done something. That is the expectation. The expectation is not that you are going to try and resolve this issue so it doesn't happen again. The expectation is that you are going to punish them.

This is Mr. Espada's second administration in three years in this school and he is able to see how administration impacts discipline. According to him, the principal sets the tone for discipline. The principal has to be clear and consistent; this was not the case with the previous administration.

The old one, principal, wanted to see a lot of the students succeed so there were a lot of students who were negatively impacting the school that she was trying to save. She tried to save them at the expense of the school as a whole, or the culture of the school as a whole because there was a perception of favoritism. And I can't think of any one word that would really destroy any type of culture that you are going to do in the high school, and that is favoritism. As long as students feel that everybody is in the same boat, they will buy into whatever you have got. But if you see some people are getting away with other things, and it is okay for them but you are not, you are dead.

Mr. Espada admits that it will be difficult to change the culture. Teachers have to be trained and held accountable, students need consistent enforcement of the discipline code, and the principal has to be visible. "It's a multiyear process . . . the trick is that every year you set the stage for the next year." The challenge lies in working with several cohorts of students at the same time—the incoming class, who are impressionable, and the upper termers, who saw a different administration's discipline policy.

Mr. Espada (C2S4D) gives the freshmen a lot of attention with the hopes that they will positively affect the next cohort. He believes that discipline is "high" on the new principal's agenda and it will move the school in the right direction.

CONCLUSION

Looking at the schools as independent and individual entities separate and apart from the campus provides an opportunity to see the commitment of principal and teachers to see their school succeed. More importantly, it allows us to see how important the principals' leadership is to making the small schools work.

One of the challenges the principals faced in maintaining discipline was getting the teachers to take equal responsibility for that process. It is easy to understand why some teachers have more difficulty with discipline then others. When a teacher has a full program, is responsible for covering a specific curriculum, and is accountable for the results, it can become overwhelming, especially for the younger and inexperienced teacher.

A teacher in NYCDOE can teach as many as 170 students in any given day (five classes with thirty-four students in each class). Without the dedicated time and reduced teaching load, teachers cannot get to know their students and effectively deal with discipline problems. The one school that required teachers to address behavioral problems as part of a team experienced greater teacher turnover than the other small schools on the campus.

Regardless of the involvement of the teachers or the shared leadership perspective of the school, the principal's leadership was the most important element in establishing discipline and creating a safe learning environment. The deans indicated that the principal must be "visible" and "set the tone," and that discipline must be "high on the agenda."

It is interesting to note that the climate in the school was reflective of the principal's personality and his/her previous administrative experience. For example, Dr. Alvarado's high expectation for student behavior and her "no-nonsense" approach to discipline was clearly articulated to students and staff, which was necessary for a school of six hundred.

Mr. Girgenti's calm and strong presence was instrumental in helping his staff gain control of a school that was losing their battle with discipline. His previous administrative and organizational experience was also valuable in creating a climate conducive to learning. In the case of Ms. DeGioulis, her "maternal but firm" approach was ideal for a small school of 370 students.

On the other hand, Mr. Lipchitz's "hands-off" approach to discipline was creating some friction among the staff, so much so that the school was experiencing a higher turnover than the other schools. In this case his lack of previous administrative and organizational experience may have led him astray in his understanding of discipline practices appropriate for his school size or staff capacity to handle behavioral problems.

In addition, his desire to not add additional support, such as assistant principal or dean, created undue stress for teachers, who were already dealing with a population that lacked command of the English language. By his own admission, Mr. Lipchitz indicated that his school was known as a "loud" school, although it did not seem to bother him.

Building a more positive, safer, and welcoming school requires effort, even in smaller learning environments. Although in this case some of the schools were quite large for a "small school." With the exception of one school that had 370 students, most of them had over 450 students and one had 600 students. That may be small by NYC's large-school standard, but nevertheless they were still large enough that they required a concerted effort to create and maintain a safe and orderly environment. It also required the principals to have a visible role in creating that environment.

The leadership of the principal was key in creating a culture in the school that gave voice to teachers' and students' concerns, helped teachers develop a relationship with their students, and provided a structure that supported those endeavors. And although not all the teachers had the same understanding of discipline as their principals, they continued to work together to create a safe environment.

However, this sentiment of working together regardless of individual understandings did not translate well for the council. The principals' leadership was still being tested as they encountered the one thing they were not trained to do: work collaboratively with other principals to manage a campus and to ensure it remained safe and secure.

The Principals' Council would have to decide collectively on how to best manage the campus by sharing facilities and using their combined resources. It may have sounded simple at the beginning, but it turned out to be one of the most difficult aspects of residing on a campus—and one that challenged their leadership skills.

Chapter 3

Collaborative Leadership
The Inner Workings of a Principals' Council

The closing of a school due to underperformance and violence may not be the ideal context to start up a school, but it was the circumstance that all the schools confronted. The challenges were numerous: hostility from the phase-out school; student violence; negative perceptions from the community; safety agents with negative attitudes; and countless restructurings from the central administration.

Eight years later, the principals feel that the building is the safest it has been since the phaseout of the large school. The closing of the school brought closure to the process. The schools are doing well, although some have fared better than others that have experienced multiple changes in leadership. The process was difficult for the campuses, but one that they all embraced.

As the principals continued to work on developing their schools, they were also entrusted with the additional responsibility of managing a campus. The NYCDOE established the Principals' Council (PLC in some buildings) on each campus to facilitate the process. The campus Principals' Council was created to ensure that all principals had equal rights and responsibilities in the decision-making process regarding issues that impact the campus.

The NYCDOE called it the "locus of control." The theory behind the "locus of control" concept is that the people closest to the problems are able to make a better decision; hence, a campus that is well managed creates opportunities and conditions for success. Implied in this statement is the understanding that there is, or must be, a strong working relationship among the members of the council, and that its members will abide by its decisions.

The Principals' Council consists of experienced and educated professionals who believe strongly in the teaching and learning process and are committed to the academic success of their students. They engage in continuous decision making that reflects their commitment for student achievement. As building administrators they are in the position to understand what is best for their schools. The same can be said about campus schools' principals; they are in the position to determine what is best for the campus.

This commonality provides a unique starting point for the principals to agree on the desirable state for the campus. All other decisions will stem from this valued end. The ability to reach consensus or how to reach that valued end still challenges the councils and totally eludes others. Although lack of training may account for some of the dysfunction, the primary reason for the council's failure to reach consensus was its inability to reconcile the dichotomous understanding of autonomy and collective.

Principals have been empowered with autonomy to do what is best for their schools. They can reach those decisions on their own or they can have input from other sources such as faculty, staff, students, and parents. On the other hand, campus principals have a responsibility—not the option—of deciding what is best for the campus and then making it happen. The campus community depends on the principals making the right decision. This requires consensus.

An effective Principals' Council requires a solid foundation starting with its legitimacy. Legitimacy is not a concept discussed much in education unless the conversation revolves around a law or regulation that mandates compliance. Yet legitimacy plays an important role in the governance of the Principals' Council and how it reaches consensus. It is the recognition of its authority. Legitimacy makes the council responsible and accountable for its decisions; without it, the council will have difficulty reaching consensus.

Governance will dictate how the principals reach consensus. It is where autonomy and collective converge. And it can only be reached through the collaborative leadership of the principals. Collaborative leadership is complex and it requires a prerequisite set of skills: relationship building, sharing control, and mediating and negotiating in good faith. Although these skills are not new to school leadership, they do take on a new meaning when interacting with individuals that have the same level of authority, as is the case with the principals on a campus.

The concepts of legitimacy, autonomy versus collective, and collaborative leadership will be explored through the Principals' Council on the two campuses. The Marin and Cuomo Campuses provide an opportunity to learn from their struggles and challenges; the sources of conflict; and a potential framework for collaborative work among school leaders in campus settings.

PRINCIPALS' COUNCIL LEGITIMACY

When we think about partnerships we usually think of a collaborative agreement between two or more parties. There is a mutual understanding that their combined efforts will produce the desired outcomes. The partnership has a legitimate reason for its existence and therefore will adhere to its contractual agreement. But more importantly, the partners will support each other in order to ensure successful and potentially profitable outcome.

Unfortunately, the Principals' Council did not have such an auspicious beginning. The council was more of an "arranged" partnership. The schools were selected on the basis of criteria determined by central administration that included building location, borough or district, superintendent's requests, and potential demand. Since each new school had a founder, the principals' potential for collaborative work was not a factor in the decision.

In fact, the principals' ability to work in and with a particular community was never considered. And since the mix of principals on the campus was never a factor in the decision-making process, the resulting "council" was a group of individuals that had no clear understanding of their role in the partnership or how it was suppose to work. Who's in charge? How are decisions made? What happens if we don't agree?

In essence, the council authority, its legitimacy, was in question. Legitimacy refers to its social acceptability and credibility (Scott, 2001). The question that begs to be asked is where does the council's legitimacy come from. Is it bestowed on it by the power of the central administration (laws, regulatory)? Is it by agreement of the members to pursue valued ends through conceptions of fair practices (values, normative)? Or is it a socially constructed framework of meaning where any decision made outside of this construction is inconceivable or inappropriate (cultural)?

The establishment of the Principals' Council has been mandated by the central administration. Its role is to shape the educational environment so that it is conducive to teaching and learning through the communication and collaboration of its members. The council has no regulatory authority to mandate any member to comply with the decisions it makes—a definite shortsightedness from central administration. From a regulatory perspective, the council is a toothless lion. With no power to sanction any of its members or force them to comply, it serves as a "special committee" that can only recommend.

In the absence of a regulatory power, the authority of some councils comes from its norms and values. Normative systems are based on norms and values created or adopted within the council. Norms are prescriptive, specifying how things should be done. Values indicate a preferred state, what is desirable. Normative systems define goals, the means to achieve them, and how to assess them. The stated beliefs are incorporated in its governance and intended outcomes. These are norms and values that all members are expected to subscribe to (Scott, 2001).

Ideally, Principals' Councils should work from a shared value and belief system. Shared values, belief, assumptions, and experiences create the framework for a cultural-cognitive system. Social reality is conceptualized through interaction and experiences within the collective; meaning is discussed and negotiated. Compliance is achieved through the belief systems of its members that any other behavior is unacceptable or inappropriate. This cultural-cognitive state may not be a far-fetched concept.

The power of culture is a reality that all principals live with on a daily basis, whether it's understanding the neighborhood laws by which the students live by or the way teachers work in the school. "This is the way we do things" is more important than any mandate. Councils that work at this level don't need central administration to legitimize their existence to function effectively and efficiently. However, this is not an easy state to reach, nor is it for the faint of heart.

The legitimacy of the council is granted one of two ways: the principals collectively agree on governance of the council, or by decree by central administration. In NYC, the Department of Education (DOE) has mandated the establishment of a Principals' Council but it has provided very little guidance on its governance. The role of central administration will be discussed in a separate section but for now we can say that its approach to campus governance has been anything but helpful.

GOVERNANCE

The decisions made by the principals, individually and collectively, ultimately impact the campus. Therefore the results of those decisions, good or bad, will depend on the strength of the relationship among the principals. However, a partnership that is forged in the midst of turmoil may not result in the ideal relationship. For the campus principals in the phase-out schools, closing a large, underperforming, and violent school, and starting new small schools was not conducive to creating a strong and cohesive council.

It's been established that the Principals' Council was created to ensure that all principals had equal rights and responsibilities in the decision-making process regarding issues that impact the campus—not the individual schools. The individual schools are under the jurisdiction of the principals. Nevertheless, it's important to remember that the individual schools make up the campus. This is where the relationship becomes symbiotic.

This is a critical understanding for the campus principals and an important step for developing the formal and informal decision-making processes that the council will engage in. The principal is responsible for his or her school but the school lives in a community (campus) of schools. This community would not exist if there weren't any schools. Therefore it is the responsibility of all the schools to be responsible for the safety and prosperity of the community.

Once the principals are clear about this symbiotic relationship, they can then decide on the best approach to making decisions; that is, creating protocols for governance. The first step is to reach an understanding on how agreements will be reached, whether it's by consensus or majority or quorum or even "drawing straws." Or maybe a combination of methods will be less taxing on the principals.

The council may decide that not all decisions require the energy of all the principals. The council would then need to determine the who, when, and why of the decision that needs to be made. If one of the principals is the point person for the athletic department, then that principal should make the day-to-day decisions of running the sports program. On the other hand, if a new team is being advocated, then the council would decide if they can afford another team, not the point principal.

But would you need consensus or the majority of the council to decide? Only the council can make that decision. The council would decide what situations or decisions require the input of all the principals. The principals have a lot on their plates and it would be an ineffective use of their time if they had to meet to make a decision on everything that impacts the campus. Therefore it is important for principals to prioritize the tasks and situations by levels. And then ensure that protocols are in place to address those problems or situations that impact the campus.

It is imperative that protocols and norms for decision making be established, even if they require tweaking and revision. And this may be the case since the partnership is organic. There is movement in and out of the council. Every principal that leaves and every new principal installed changes the dynamic of the council to some degree. However, transitioning of new principals would be less chaotic because "if it's done correctly, and you're building that legacy of professional learning and growth as a campus, the person should fit in seamlessly, with training," explained Dr. Alvarado. She elaborated:

> I think if you're doing it correctly, you're building a legacy as time goes on. So if one of the players is removed from the process, you still have those, you know, initial team members who are part of it. So they're the ones that should be able to support the new administration, the newbie to the block, and making sure that, you know, they're fair, and they're honest, and they're transparent about the process, and show them how it's done. And if they have a new perspective to bring to the table, they should do that too.

Creating protocols and establishing norms is one of the most difficult tasks any partnership can engage in because all the parties have to agree on them. In an arranged partnership like the Principals' Council it may be easier if the consensus-building process is facilitated by an outside consultant or organization rather than internally, therefore avoiding the perception of bias. This process proved to be beneficial for the principals on the Cuomo Campus, according to Mr. Messiah.

> And it was a very intense retreat. It was at the University of Penn. So we learned . . . about team dynamics, about goal setting, about doing the right thing. And then we had another piece about team building was on—about protocols. And one of the things that they did, that's still fresh in my mind, is the "360 evaluations." You know, how your supervisor thinks about you, and how your colleagues and your subordinates think of you, and how the circle completes itself, and how true it was with several of us. . . . It was like, "Wow. It's amazing."

Consensus building and creating protocols, however, is a long process and requires continuous follow-up. Cutting the process short to save money will only sabotage the process and damage the fragile bond between the principals, which is what happened with the Marin Campus council.

> We had a coach who came in and he met with us. And we also went on a retreat. And he would, you know, helps us work out our issues, you know, try to move forward. But that kind of died down. And people didn't—I mean people, yes, continued bickering. But they became less responsible for the campus and saw it as just a building where I have my school in, but very little campus unity. (Dr. Alvarado)

Unfortunately, the repercussions were long lived with this council. A deeper look into the areas that cause the most disruptions on the campus show that it stemmed from the council itself. One principal lamented:

> They basically don't want to work together right now. And you know that's why I say the model that we are following, I believe, will never work unless the people, the principals, that are in the group learn to collaborate and give and take a little bit. . . .

If it's all about playing well in the sandbox, you'll find out that in most of these campus schools, they don't. And central is aware of it. (Mr. Girgenti)

Undoubtedly getting everyone to play well in the sandbox will require that all the principals realize that they are equal partners in this relationship and therefore have equal responsibilities for its success. The solution to the problems of the council will have to come from the principals themselves. The good news is once the council has agreed in its governance half the battle is won. Confusion is eliminated or at least seriously reduced. The authority levels are clear and so is the accountability.

Accountability is the results of good governance. Good governance dictates that agreements are well articulated and understood by all parties and that everyone will abide by those agreements (Archer & Cameron, 2013). That is why governance is so important; it legitimizes the authority of the partnership. It infers that individuals will take responsibilities for their role and for the success of the partnership. Unfortunately, creating an accountability system is as just as hard as consensus building.

Accountability means that someone is held responsible for an action or failure to take action. More importantly, it implies that there are consequences for the decisions taken and/or the results for said decision. The question the council then faces is "What possible consequences can a principal suffer as a result of failing to meet their obligation? This question was a source of frustration among the council members.

> If one school says, "You know what? I did my budgeting, I don't have any money," who's to say that she needs to contribute, or he needs to contribute to what was agreed upon? And that's the stuff that drives me crazy. You agreed to one thing and, then once you leave, you change things. We're no one. We can't tell them anything. (Mr. Messiah)

Unfortunately, this question cannot be answered with a simple "if-then." For one thing, the Principals' Council is not a voluntary partnership; it is imposed and therefore it cannot be dissolve by the council, so removing principals is not an option. Second, all principals have the same level of authority and therefore cannot discipline a peer. So what's a council to do? There's a bigger question here, "Why would a principal renege on his/her responsibilities?"

That's the question that needs to be asked to the principal in question. If the principal is given the benefit of doubt, then the door is open for an honest conversation about the problem. There could be a valid reason for not meeting his obligation. And that principal deserves the opportunity to explain the situation. If the situation is out of his/her control then the council—together—should find an alternative solution.

However, if the situation arose out of the principal's negligence, incompetence, or spitefulness, then the conversation changes. And yet what consequences can a principal face as a result of not meeting his/her obligation and responsibilities? Depending on the severity of the infraction, the council may decide to keep it internally or take it out to central.

The council does not impose penalties in a traditional sense. The principal is not fined or benched. However, breaking the trust given to the principals is a serious offense with long-lasting repercussions. The council may decide that there are certain programs that they will no longer involve the offending principal in. It can be costly for the principal, not just in expenses but the lost resources to his school.

Many campuses share programs, teachers, summer school, and partnerships with CBO. These programs or collaborations are created by the council and are not part of the mandated cost that each school has to cover. The collaboration creates economies of scale and more opportunities for students. Losing one or all of these resources can cause incredible hardship for any school. The principal would have to figure out how to fund or replace the lost resource.

There are situations that are beyond the council's ability to resolve, such as in the case where a principal refuses to pay his share of campus cost. This requires the intervention of central administration or the superintendent. Calling in the cavalry does have its drawbacks; it exposes the council to outsiders and it can expose other areas that the council would like to keep under the radar. And if it's not done correctly it can leave some hard feelings that can resurface in council dealings.

AUTONOMY OR COLLECTIVE

For the most part, principals consider themselves to be autonomous. In their mind they can make any decision they feel is necessary for their school. However, when you are on a campus there could be potential impact to the building. For example if the principal decides to reduce staff members that supervise students the campus will be impacted, since students will find themselves in other schools' space or in shared spaces. The potential for mischievousness or violence is high without adult supervision. The problem has now become a campus problem.

The following is a perfect example of a decision made without regard to its impact on the campus. The problem at hand was a change of the bell schedule by one school at the Marin Campus. The campus had always had one bell schedule (as most campuses do) that facilitated the use of shared space, such as gyms and cafeterias. However, one principal decided to change the bell schedule for his school.

The principal assumed that the change would not impact the other schools since his school had its own gym space. The school's lunch period would be the starting point for the rest of the schedule since it is a fixed period. Unfortunately, the principal either neglected or decided to disregard the impact the start time and ending of his school day had on the rest of the campus. The school's first period now began fifteen minutes after the campus's start time, resulting in traffic after everyone was settled in class.

Students that came early were mulling around because the school did not assign a place for them to go or personnel to attend to them. The change of classes was also problematic when students had to cross another school's space. Unfortunately, this principal did not account for how this change would affect the rest of the campus or if there were systems in place to deal with the challenges resulting from the bell change. The PLC was not informed of this decision prior to its implementation. One principal commented, "It took autonomy to the next level."

> If I wanted to change our bell schedule here, I would like to think that we'd do it in such a way that it doesn't affect anyone else. Right? And if, in fact, my students weren't where they were supposed to be and disrupting another class or the flow of the building, I would have to address it. You see? Because why would you change that schedule simply because maybe you need a longer period for math and you want to do it a period and a half rather than you know [a period], or shorten a day. I mean, you have oh so many options. But you know, you're living with five other schools, so you need to put that into place. And then, if you are able to do that without affecting or distracting anyone else, and that you take care of, you know, the knucklehead children that won't listen to or won't follow those kinds of rules, then you have to listen to the other schools if, in fact, they are being disruptive. (Mr. Girgenti)

For many campus principals, being a collective means you are not autonomous, that one negates the other. And it is easy to understand this myth. In NYC the Bloomberg administration advocated competition and autonomy so that the principal could be held accountable. As a result, collaboration, cooperation, and consensus building were not required.

Unfortunately, multiple principals were placed in one building and asked to do just that: collaborate, cooperate, and reach consensus. The principals were now truly confused. How do they compete and collaborate? How do they become a collective but still be autonomous? It's the age-old question of how not to lose yourself in a relationship.

Partnership collaboration lies in a continuum from an interdependent (symbiotic) "we stand together, we fall together" relationship to a shared "I bring, you bring" relationship. There is also a contractual "I pay, you produce" type of relationship. And like any continuum, there are shades in between. Regardless of where the relationship is in the continuum, clarity of purpose and transparency will dictate its success.

Setting aside the fact that campus principals do not choose the campus they want to be in—although that would be preferable—there is no reason to believe that this "arranged" partnership should not work. The key to its success lies in understanding the purpose of the relationship, what it takes to achieve the stated goals, and where in the collaboration continuum you need to be in order to achieve said goals. In a campus school, that collaboration can move within the continuum. The reason why it can do that is because it's situational. The best way to explain this is via examples.

In a symbiotic relationship both parties will benefit or suffer together. On a campus, if one school has an uncontrollable gang problem it will easily translate to a campus problem. Because in the gang world, no "disrespect or injury" will go unpunished. And it doesn't matter if the incident was at school or in the neighborhood. There will be retaliation. The question is, "How explosive will the situation get and can it be contained? Better yet, do we have enough information about the potential problem so that we can be proactive and derail it?"

Communication among schools will be very important when addressing interschool conflicts. Any unresolved issue between students in one school will grow and eventually impact the other schools on the campus. Mr. Messiah recalls a school problem that became a campus problem:

> For example, we had a big incident in the building with Black and Spanish girls. Huge! It was big, you know, going on for a year, almost a year and a half in one particular school. And then other schools started jumping along. And before we knew it, it was like—wait a minute—this was all new, or new to us; but not new to that school.

The schools had to come together to address the situation as a campus. They brought in organizations that focused on the issues at hand and tightened their security protocols. However, if the principal of the school had worked with the council this problem would have been avoided. Unfortunately, the principal did not want the other principals to know the problem or the scale of the problem and tried to keep it under the radar with dire results.

And even if a school does not have a gang problem, there are many other situations that can arise in any given day. Consider the fact that an average high school can have anywhere between five hundred and thousand students in its register. If you have five or six schools in a building the total population can swell to twenty-five hundred or three thousand students. The odds of a student having a family member or a friend in one of the other schools on the campus are very high.

And equally high are the odds that they will have an enemy on the campus. The potential for problems are always high and that's just internal. External problems are a whole different ball game. When it comes to safety and the security of the school building, only a symbiotic relationship will work. The council has to work as a collective.

In a shared relationship, where there is a mutual agreement, each of the parties brings an expertise or a resource to the table or decides to work together on a project because either economies of scale makes it easier to fund or it will benefit the entire student population. A college fair is a perfect example of a mutual partnership. College representatives prefer to attend fairs at schools with the greatest number of potential candidates.

So the likelihood that the schools will get representatives increases with the number of students (all other factors being equal). Campuses where the principals have agreed to sponsor a fair together have seen a greater response and more broad representation of colleges, benefiting all students. However, there are campuses that refuse to do campus fairs and prefer to do their own little fair.

Other than the fact that it seems selfish and counterintuitive, there is one more reason why this is detrimental to campus morale. Not every school functions effectively or at full capacity, for a myriad of reasons such as poor leadership, shortage of personnel, and shortage of funds, to name a few. Nevertheless these should not be reasons enough for the students in that school not to have the same opportunities as the other schools on the campus. That alone should be reason enough to work together on an event.

Of course there are a number of opportunities for the campus to share resources, such as agreeing to fund a music or arts program. The shortage of a teacher provides the opportunity for a school to partially pay for a teacher in another school to teach the students part-time. Collaborating on a RFP to bring a program to the school is a wonderful opportunity for campus staff to work together. If we think about the impact that schools have on students' lives there shouldn't be a reason for creative use of resources within the campus.

Contractual relationships also have their place in a campus setting. On many campuses there are shared personnel. These individuals usually serve either in a clerical capacity or as school aides but are paid and supervised by one school. In these situations, the supervising school handles any conflict this staff has with any of the schools on the campus.

There are pros and cons to this type of relationship. On the positive side, it's one less person the principal has to supervise or pay. That's always good. And you get free labor. What more can you ask for? Though, it does get a little complicated when conflicts and complaints do not get addressed on a timely basis or if the principal favors the employee. However, this too can be resolved with a little bit of negotiation and collaboration.

In each of the above examples, the members of the council have worked together to support the goal of a safe and orderly environment that is conducive to teaching and learning. In the end, it's not about whether you're collective or autonomous but rather what the situation dictates. When the principals understand the range of collaboration on a campus they'll feel less threatened by the collective concept in a Principals' Council.

COLLABORATIVE LEADERSHIP

Collaborative leadership is complex by nature but more so when the partnership is arranged and not entered voluntarily. There are several skills that are critical in a collaborative setting such as a campus school. One of them is the ability to build relationships and resolve the inevitable conflict that stems from the relationship (Archer & Cameron, 2013). The principals on the campus placed an enormous emphasis on the skills that a leader brings to the campus, not so much work experience but the ability to work with people:

> You know, how they [principals] present ideas. Do they listen well? These are all things that are important to observe in a leader in the campus situation. . . . But I think personality is a key. And sometimes you can't change people's personalities or their belief systems. But I think it has to be expected of principals that come into a campus. And a lot of these schools that are growing, that are new schools, I think it has to be made very clear to them, that you're going into a campus structure. And these are our expectations. And maybe sign off on them, like a contract. (Dr. Rodriguez)

Another principal commented on the importance of "Besides a skin of Teflon . . . really highly qualified managerial skills where you learn how to manage different teams, and you learn that what works for one may not work for the other." One principal presented an interesting analogy:

> And those skills are: knowing how to get along with the other principals, knowing that we are colleagues, all on the same playing field, having the same responsibilities as well as the same wish that their schools can progress at a steady pace, that the good things are able to be maintained, and that we work together for them [students]. And not walk away from issues that affect everyone. Because it's like the kid on the playground who owns the bat and the ball, and walks away and ends the game. That's not good. We need to all play together. All our equipment—put all our equipment together. And still have different teams, but one league. (Dr. Alvarado)

Being on a campus requires more "maturity and discipline," reflected Ms. DeGioulis because the "learning curve is steep." More importantly, "Leave your ego at the door, which is very difficult for new principals to do," stated Mr. Messiah. There is no doubt that being a collaborative leader requires special skills. It is "one of the most sophisticated and mature styles of leadership" as it requires leaders to have the skills to build relationships, share control, and mediate and negotiate in good faith.

The *number one* cause for dysfunctional councils is the lack of maturity and experience of some of its members: a prevalent trait of the principals that came to power during the Bloomberg administration. Almost 80 percent of NYC principals came to the principalship during this era; 20 percent of them were under forty years old and had less than five years of teaching experience under their belt (Siskin, 2011). Many had no school-building experience either. They were "knighted" and "empowered" and placed on a campus. There were some big personalities in these councils.

> But certainly, the personalities, if they're not going to be cooperative or their personality doesn't let them go the next step. Maturity-wise, you know, younger principals, I feel, have a much more difficult time than those that have experience in the classroom, and dealing with administration as a whole, definitely.... There is something to say about being in education a long time, and knowing how to work with people, as opposed to coming in and having the kind of power that they have, and using it loosely. (Mr. Messiah)

Although we've established the fact that it is possible to be autonomous and still have a collective interest, it may not be so easy for all principals. As one principal on the campus exclaimed, "If I die and go to hell, I want to be put in a campus!" Such an emotional outburst, although uncommon in public, may be descriptive of some campus principals' feelings about campus life.

Principals must be willing to communicate and be able to articulate clearly their understanding about issues at hand. Consider how different the outcome of the incident where the principal changed the bell schedule of his school would have been if he had taken the time to communicate his plan. The problem was not that he changed his schedule, only that he failed to consider the impact on the campus.

Had this principal communicated his intention to the council, the principals would have brainstormed the potential impact on the campus and discussed possible solutions. This collaborative effort would have ensured a smoother transition from one schedule to another. The principal then would continue with his modification to his instructional program without impacting the other schools' instructional program.

Collaboration is difficult. It takes more energy to work interdependently than to work independently. Building relationships means you need to take time to know and understand your partners. You need to mediate the conflicts that arise from sharing control and accountability. You have to confer, convey, exchange, and discuss; that is, you need to communicate continuously. But equally important is the quality of the communication.

Communication that is not transparent creates distrust. You cannot build a relationship without trust; not "blind trust" but rather the "good faith" trust that dictates honesty in conversation and transparency in negotiation. Otherwise everyone will be out for him or herself and never consider the other parties. As one principal commented, "The fights get ugly when people are not transparent."

ASSIGNED SCHOOL SPACE

Assigned space on a campus is premier real estate holding and as such it must be preserved at all cost. Keeping valuable space meant that some principals got "creative" about its use and purpose. Some principals would "create classes" to explain space utilization or attach specific space requirements to their theme-based school in order to justify their allotment of space without considering the current or evolving needs of the campus or the schools within it.

> They feel that they have ownership of those classrooms. They don't want to give them up. "My program is more important than your program." "I am the A school." "I am the one that teaches Spanish, French [and] Chinese. I need these three." "I am the one with five AP classes, you know." And yes, they're right. But I think there's a better way to manage that and deal with that. But I need you to be transparent. I need you to be able to say, "You know what? I can afford to give up a classroom." (Mr. Messiah)

However, all this creativity comes at cost. "I wish we could get along a little better. We're not getting along," reflected one principal, lamenting the current state of the council. In fact, the animosity among some of the principals on the Marin Campus is so palpable that some of the council meetings are not just heated—they're hostile. "I actually get stomach cramps when I have to go to these," one principal confessed. Speaking about a recent PLC meeting, the principal described a scene that evolved before them:

> But today, the conflict was between two other principals. And, you know, the anger in their faces is very disheartening for me. And all I tried to do is actually try to divert the attention away from that [the issue] to me, and the issue at hand. And I find that sometimes I'm unsuccessful because they just have a history of bitterness. (Mr. Girgenti)

As a result there is continuous bickering and the decision-making process is a formidable task. Until there is a resolution among the principals to work past the negative history, the council will continue to struggle in its efforts to become a community. Dr. Alvarado reflected:

> And, you know, it doesn't seem as if we're working toward a more—learning community. It still seems very much your school is on the third floor and my school is on the first floor. We'll see each other every once in a while. There have been efforts made. But every time, and any time we hit a roadblock or a challenge, it becomes, again, the isolated way of thinking, the isolate's way of thinking. (Dr. Alvarado)

Continued animosity and distrust among the principals hampers every attempt they make to negotiate and find solutions. And worse of all it allows for the continuation of inequities that impact the schools—impact students. "As principals, we tend to be very territorial," explained Ms. DeGioulis. "They have ownership of their space and will not give it up unless it is mandated, despite the negative impact it has on another school."

> I have one bathroom for all my students. I don't have laboratories. I don't have self-contained rooms. I don't have a teacher workstation. You know, there's so many things that we don't have, that in real schools, or fully equipped schools, this would have been a non-issue. I mean, chemistry lab. We have these little mobile labs that we have to move, with Bunsen burners. This is 2010. We are a world leader. We shouldn't have to be fighting over "Can I have access to your laboratory?" Those are issues that really will impede the educational success of our students, I think. (Ms. DeGioulis)

The space allocation continued to be a glaring problem that was not going away. And yet it didn't have to be that way. In true collaborative fashion, Mr. Messiah had suggested that the entire campus be reconfigured. "Let's move the schools around," he recommended. It would have been a monumental task to reconfigure the campus. Negotiations would have gone on potentially for weeks, months, or maybe an entire school year, but in the end there would have been an equitable distribution of space. Unfortunately, that idea did not sit well with some of the principals.

On the Marin Campus, the fear of losing space was at the center of a major conflict experienced by the council. One of the principals, not the founding principal of the school, believed that they were given less space than they were entitled to from the beginning. He believed that the founding principal was not aware or did not understand the space distribution process and, therefore, did not ask for additional space. "But the space was not given out equitably when the phase-out school closed out a year ago. And we got zero and the other schools got something," the principal explained.

"There is one school that had five too many classrooms. One had three too many. One had one too many," the principal argued. However, solving this problem would require the redistribution of space that has belonged to a school for years, possibly since its inception. Although the council has been told that they can reconfigure the space if the principals agree to it, it's unlikely to happen. "Do you really think people are going to agree to give up part of their school?" asked Mr. Lipchitz.

The principal with less space tried negotiating with the principals in the adjoining space but when that failed he then presented his case to the council. Despite the repeated request of the principal to correct the space allocation, the council was unsuccessful in resolving this issue. As a result, it became necessary to involve the networks and central administration's facilities personnel to resolve the dispute, though some of the principals believed it was unnecessary to take this out of the building. Measuring his words carefully one principal stated:

> Now, ideally, again, the PLC should be the ones who handle all this without going out. So, there's a protocol, you know; it's been broken. I think when this issue of the rooms was done, where one school went to you know . . . sent out messages outside of the building about how . . . it involved them [central administration and the networks] unnecessarily. And, I think, prematurely. But they wanted to get their point across. And I thought it was not a healthy thing for our PLC. It sort of made us, you know, a little upset with each other, I think. (Dr. Rodriguez)

The appealing principal disagreed. According to the principal, the issue of space allocation had already been brought to the council during the previous school year. It reached a point where unpleasant e-mails were being exchanged:

> And I said, "You're surprised because the e-mail that you see on the bottom of this thing clearly states we'd be going to the next level" because he didn't help, he didn't accommodate me. I said, as it is now, I have three teachers teaching six period coverages because I don't have a place to place another teacher in my school if I wanted to hire one. You know, they don't have answers for these things. (Mr. Girgenti)

After a year of conversations and procrastination, the principal decided to take it to the next level:

> And it had to go through the networks, then facilities. And facilities came in and we had numbers. And it's unfortunate because, you know, some people had to lose space and some people gained space. . . . I was happy with what occurred. And every year, though, we have to revisit this. . . . But, see, all of this could be solved.

The principal is right. It could have been solved, avoiding all the drama that came with the solution. In this case the principal tried negotiating with neighboring principals and when that didn't work he took it to the council. For a whole year this principal tried to get the council to address the issue of space inequity, to no avail. Unfortunately, the only recourse was to take it outside of the council. But more importantly, the damage to the partnership was costly and it only added fuel to a strained relationship.

BUDGET WOES

Just like space, budget negotiations challenge the council. Negotiation that involves money is a difficult task for anyone but for a council that is not united, it is a daunting task. It is easy to understand why money-talk is difficult for a principal. The demands are great and the resources are limited. Add to that the demands of the campus and it can get overwhelming. And believe it or not a campus does have expenses. These will be discussed in the chapter Under New Management. However, it is important to note that the council does not receive additional funds to pay for campus expenses.

The economies of scale that large schools operated under allowed for the cost of certain personnel, like an assistant principal of operations. However, the budget of a small school does not allow for such luxuries. In fact, if you combine the budget of five small schools you still would not get the benefit of scale of one large school because the budgets are calculated separately by school and not by campus. Nevertheless, central administration, in its infinite wisdom, left it for the schools to figure out how to address the problem of campus expenses.

Since a school's budget is driven by student register, a decrease in enrollment will be reflected in the lost revenue associated with that decrease. Schools are also impacted by the economy. Federal, state, and city allotment per student can rise and fall as a direct response to the economy. In turn, schools have to allocate their resources differently; hence campuses have to allocate their contributing funds differently. Meeting the obligations of their schools and still being responsible for the financial needs of the campus is overwhelming for many small-school principals.

Budget issues are difficult conversations at the PLC. The biggest issue is who will be paying for key staff members. Mr. Messiah explains that decisions to pay for staff can change due to register loss, however, the campus does not receive any directions on how to solve this problem. He illustrates the conversation among the principals:

> Right now, we're going through a budget crisis, where one school says, "I don't have any register. I don't have the money to pay." And we're not talking about per session [overtime]; we're not talking about supplies. We're talking about salary. When that person is in someone's TO [table of organization] and now needs to be somewhere else, who's going to pick that up? Who's going to volunteer to say, "I need this?" No one is. So, what's going to happen to that person? (Mr. Messiah)

In light of the difficult economy and its impact on schools' budgets, the principals' decision to pay their share of expenses has been challenging.

Nevertheless, the campus has expenses and the schools have to meet those obligations regardless of the economic situation or the schools' budget. However, that is easier said than done since you can't force a principal to contribute. Mr. Girgenti explained the process:

> And when one school refuses to pay their fair share, no matter how you present the information, and then what are your recourses? And the recourses that are set up are to bring your network in, and then go through this whole process. Instead of working collaboratively and in the best interest of the campus, we make agreements; and some schools don't follow through.

The issue of accountability continues to challenge the councils. Some of the members are torn between taking the problem to another level or living with the frustration of unresolved problems. However, the recourse available may not be the best solution if the principals are not in agreement on going through the process, as in the case of the Marin Campus. While the outcome did benefit the petitioning school, some of the other principals (the ones affected) believe that it was not a "healthy thing" for the council. The displeasure caused by the outcome was another "sore" in the council.

In all the examples provided so far, the underlying problem stems from the council itself: the clarity of its purpose, the quality and transparency in its decision-making process, and its accountability to the members. In other words, the legitimacy of the partnership is unclear. The issue of legitimacy has to be resolved before any council can function correctly.

Either the council is accountable to its members because it is mandated to do so or because anything less would be unacceptable. Although some high-performing councils have been able to legitimize their governance on their own, it is mainly due to the collaborative leadership of the principals involved. Unfortunately, this has not been the norm on many campuses.

CONCLUSION

Much has been written about the difficulties of addressing inequities in society, however, for educators, the issue of equity should be nonnegotiable. How can a principal work, in good conscience, in a building with twice the amount of space for the same number of students, knowing that a colleague has to use Bunsen burners to teach chemistry? Or for that matter, the issue of whether or not a principal will pay their share of campus expenses and potentially put the safety and security of the campus in question.

Collaborative leaders on a campus work from a value-end perspective, but it is informed by ongoing and continuous knowledge construction (cultural-cognitive). The cultural-cognitive perspective assumes a high level of socially mediated construction. Legitimacy that stems from this dimension comes from a deep level of understanding of the collective (shared values, beliefs, and assumptions) and its social reality (experiences and interactions) (Scott, 2001).

In its interactions, meaning is discussed and negotiated. And its compliance is achieved through the belief systems of its members that any other behavior is unacceptable or inappropriate. As difficult as it may sound to reach such a level of governance, it is possible. The key to reaching this level of governance is in understanding that socially mediated reality is constructed and not imposed.

The principals have the power to construct that reality, if they choose to. Principals are not ignorant of the power of culture in a school setting, especially those that have taken the challenge of changing one. In fact, the whole notion of changing the culture of the large school by establishing small schools was at the core of the reform. The combined effort of the principals was what was desperately needed to transform the large building.

The diversity of leadership styles, personalities, experiences, and expertise makes the Principals' Council a fertile ground for creativity and innovation. These unique qualities are reflected in each principal as they develop the culture that creates a climate that is conducive to teaching and learning in their school. These qualities combined create a powerful energy.

The principals need to channel that combined energy and use it to create a safe and orderly environment where high achievement is the norm. Co-location has many advantages despite the challenges of campus management. Among them are optimal utilization of a building, program choices for students, sharing of costs that would be prohibitive for small schools, and a pool of combined leadership talent. More importantly, the biggest advantage of co-location is the Principal's Council itself.

The principal's position is often referred to as a lonely one, regardless of a great cabinet or wonderful teachers or even school community that is comfortable with shared leadership. Difficult decisions have to be made and many require a broad perspective. It is difficult for all constituents to have a broad perspective when making decisions that impact the school.

The truth is that most teachers do not want to manage a school or micromanage decision making. Teachers want to work in safe, secure, and professional learning communities dedicated to teaching and learning and be provided with the resources needed to help their students succeed. And they also want someone who will handle the minutia of compliance and discipline and the occasional unruly, uncooperative parent.

There are decisions that only the principal can make and issues that only he or she can address. The most challenging one is staff and faculty discipline.

It is a difficult task that is made more daunting in the context of contractual and legal processes. Terminating employees due to budget cuts is another difficult decision to make. It can become overwhelming for a principal. Who does the principal talk to? Usually a principal would talk to another principal if they can find one they can trust, but that may be difficult to do when you are working in isolation or in a competitive environment.

The Principals' Council is the ideal environment for principals to decompress, to brainstorm ideas, and to seek advice. A cohesive and unified council provides the principals a "safe" place to have conversations about those difficult tasks; a place where not knowing the answers or what to do is okay. It allows the principals to interject humor in "Who does that?!" situations.

The council can also provide coaching and mentoring for newer principals. This type of on-the-job training is invaluable for newer principals and it gives the senior principals the sense of satisfaction and pride that they are supporting the next generation of school leaders. More importantly, it's a support group for both new and senior principals.

These are the types of councils that central administration should foster. Not only does this ensure that campuses are well managed, it also encourages collaboration, cooperation, and consensus building. These are important skills the school leaders need to have in today's school environments, and central administration plays an important part in developing those skills, especially in co-location situations.

Chapter 4

Under New Management
Campus Logistics and Operation

As the school leader, the principal makes the final decision on anything and everything that goes on in their school, from curriculum to books to programs. They determine how to best allocate funds to support school priorities, whether it's hiring new teachers or purchasing new equipment. Even in the most collaborative schools where there is evidence of shared leadership among the faculty, the principal is ultimately the final decision maker.

The principal's job is challenging, but being a principal in a campus setting requires a new set of skills. It requires the ability to collaborate with peers and to skillfully negotiate campus resources. To this end, the Principals' Council was created to foster a collaborative approach to decision making with regard to campus management. However, this was a challenge for the principals in the campus building as they try to balance the responsibilities of starting and developing their new schools with those of the campus.

The Cuomo Campus, consisting of six principals, and the Marin Campus, consisting of five principals, were now responsible for running two large buildings. Under consideration were overseeing safety and security personnel, coordinating the use of shared space, and managing a non-existing budget. In theory, the principals understood what they had to do. Unfortunately, it was the practical aspect of logistics and operations that was difficult. Complicating this problem was the lack of cohesiveness in the Principals' Council.

SHARED EXPENSES AND SCHOOL BUDGET

In the absence of an operations manual and with limited guidance from central administration, the council had to figure out how to deal with the logistics of campus operations. The one-school management model that was familiar to principals was the traditional operations model of large schools. In large high schools there were at least two assistant principals of administration: one for operations and one for security. Unfortunately this model was not going to work for the campus because none of the small schools would be able to afford to hire two administrators.

Most of the campus schools modified the model to substitute the assistant principals for a campus manager. This is the most expensive staff member on a campus, so much so that many campuses have forgone the luxury of having one. The campus manager is responsible for many of the duties that would have been handled by two assistant principals of administration in a traditional school: everything from mail distribution to crisis management. The campus manager relieves the principals of these administrative duties and concerns so that they can focus on their schools.

The logistics of running a campus cannot be understated. Something as simple as mail delivery can get complicated. The U.S. Post Office does not deliver mail to the individual schools; it must be delivered to a central location, sorted by school, placed in bins, and then picked up from the individual schools. Delivery of equipment and supplies is not any easier. Often goods go to the wrong school.

The campus manager is also responsible for the use of shared space. It is not unusual for two schools to show up at the auditorium at the same time because the space was not properly scheduled or because one of the principals decided that he or she needed the auditorium for an "impromptu" event. The same goes for the library. The library gets used many times as a "swing" space by the schools when there are programming conflicts or a school is short a classroom. The campus manager is responsible for coordinating these events or situations through a campus calendar, hopefully minimizing scheduling conflicts.

In addition to the administrative duties, the campus manager is responsible for the security of the building: write the campus safety plan, schedule campus safety meetings, schedule fire drills, meet with deans, coordinate campus safety with SSAs team, and lead the Building Response Team (crisis team). He is also the liaison between the police department and the schools. It is a stressful job— and expensive. The average cost for a campus manager is over $100,000 since a licensed supervisor is required for the job.

For the campus manager, it also means that he has multiple bosses. Each principal is the campus manager's immediate supervisor because they all contribute to his or her salary; however, it can get complicated because the salary only shows up in one school's budget; loyalty can get compromised. The manager may be tempted to make biased decisions in favor of the principal that has the position in their budget. On the other hand, the principal that has the position in their budget will have a huge financial burden if the other principals were to decide that they do not want to support a campus manager.

Since the campus does not receive a separate budget for shared expenses, such as the campus manager or school aides, the individual schools pay these expenses. Each school assumes a percentage of the shared expense, usually the cost of hiring the staff member that is needed on the campus. One school will hire the campus manager; another school will hire school aides that are equivalent to the cost of the manager; another will hire a librarian; and so on. All the principals contribute to the expenses associated with campus management and programs, including the very contentious PSAL program.

The athletic program or Public Schools Athletic League (PSAL) is a shared expense. The athletic program in a high school is very expensive: uniforms, equipment, transportation, and salaries. Some sports teams are less expensive to run, such as the track team, but others are extremely expensive, such as football. Depending on the number of teams on the campus the sports program can consume a good portion of the schools' budgets.

Ironically, many of the large schools that were closed had very good teams that won city and state championships. Despite the lack of academic press and violence problems, many students went to the large schools because of their sports programs. Through the athletic program many students received scholarships to college, increasing their chances of being recruited by professional teams. Unfortunately, not all the schools on a campus are committed to keeping such an expensive program.

In New York City Cost the PSAL only recognizes campus teams; individual schools on the campus are not allowed to have teams. That means that the teams continue to carry the name of the original large school that was closed. It also means that all the students, regardless of the school they went to on the campus, had equal opportunity to participate in any of the teams as long as they met participation requirements.

Since the PSAL only recognizes the campus teams, there could only be one athletic director (AD) on the campus. The AD is responsible for PSAL compliance, which means he or she must make sure that all students—on the campus—are meeting the requirements for participation. The AD must make sure that all students on campus have equal access and opportunity to participate, a difficult undertaking since schools may have different time schedules and after-school activities.

Some small schools actually discouraged—covertly—students from participating in sports by scheduling school activities during practice time. That also gave the principals of some of the small schools on the campus an excuse not to pay for the PSAL program, therefore increasing the share of the cost associated with an athletic program for the schools that want to provide students with the opportunity to participate in sports. Mr. Messiah explained the different perspectives about PSAL among the principals on the Cuomo Campus:

> But my vision about sports and athletics is different than my colleagues, which is, I want to have more teams. I'm willing to pay for uniforms. I'm willing to do all these things. Their belief is, no, what we have is fine.

Having such disparate views on the sports program creates conflict among the principals. Whereas some principals create opportunities for their students to participate in sports, others will not hesitate to discourage their kids. And since students cannot be denied participation on a team, regardless of their school's unwillingness to share in the financial commitment to the athletic program, the burden of supporting the teams will fall heavily and unfairly on some of the schools.

Those schools that bear a greater share of the cost for the sports program must rely more on fundraising events to cover expenses. However, the uncertainty of next year's budget looms large and ominous on the horizon. And because the current recourse of going outside of the building for help can cause more harm than good, the council prefers the ongoing battle to the alternative: a potential adverse rating.

Funding the PSAL program should not be at the whim of principals; however, there is a valid argument for portioning the contribution amount. It can be argued that a school with only 10 percent of its student population participating in the sports program should not pay the same amount as a school with 40 or 50 percent participation. But it can also be argued that those 10 percent have the privilege and the opportunity of participating in a program that would otherwise not exist. In fact, it may even be the reason why that student decided to go to a school on that campus.

Principals should not be excused from contributing to campus programs because of their participation rate, but they should be allowed to negotiate an equal portion of the campus expense in other services. The principal that has difficulty seeing the cost benefit of paying for a sports program that has very low participation from his school may be able to offset it with the cost of sharing an advance placement teacher with the campus.

Hiring an experienced teacher to teach an advanced placement course is expensive and difficult. The principal with the AP teacher can contribute seat-time (comparable in cost) to the other schools on the campus in lieu of contributing to the PSAL program. This can be done for any type of program, such as the arts or foreign language or even the very expensive and exclusive robotics program. It would be a win-win situation for all the schools on a campus.

Some campuses may find that their schools are not equally populated. There may be schools on the campus that have three hundred or four hundred or five hundred students. There may be even greater disparity on some campuses that have a school with a thousand students in the mist of the smaller ones. How should the share for each school be determined? Is prorate by capital? But what happens when one of the smaller schools has a greater participation in a program? Do they contribute more because their participation is higher, despite the fact that the school's budget is based on register and not participation rate?

It can get complicated very quickly and there is no easy solution or formula. There is no easy way to handle budget issues but it is important to know that there is more than one way to address it. This is where true collaboration is revealed. Fortunately, there are councils that have been able to manage to work through the money problems creatively because they have combined their collective knowledge and experience to bring solutions that will benefit the lives of their students.

Consider the campus manager position. Many campuses have forgone funding this position because the principals have decided to divide the responsibilities among themselves: One principal is the point person for security, another for facilities, another for PSAL, and so forth. Of course that means the principal will have to designate a member of his staff to take on these responsibilities. He or she may incur the expense of paying for the additional time the staff member will need to do the work, but it would be significantly less than paying for a campus manager.

The principals have to come together at the table, share the necessary information, negotiate in good faith and transparency, and reach a mutual agreement on how to share the cost of running the campus. Failure to do this will throw the council into a vortex of animosity, bickering, and distrust, resulting in a dysfunctional campus. More importantly, it will deprive students of the opportunity to participate in programs they wish to join just because the adults cannot figure it out.

SHARED SPACE AND STUDENT BEHAVIOR

The challenge that comes with coexistence is that "at times, one model will impact another." Managing students' behavior in a campus setting is demanding for the individual schools. Schools that do not have contiguous space experience more difficulty maintaining an orderly environment than schools that are self-contained. Mr. Messiah explains the impact of several schools on one floor.

> Whereas now you have three schools on one wing, one school has two classrooms; another one has two classrooms; the other one has six classrooms.

What culture are you establishing there? You have two schools with a dress code; one school without a dress code. You have two schools that are very strict; one school that could care less how the kids walk in the hallway. It's a different challenge. So what you're doing is you're mixing in all these cultures. And what you set out to do is now really challenging because your kids are learning from another school's culture. And it's more difficult to manage.

The principals in this space predicament struggle every day to develop their school's culture. This problem is compounded when the adjoining schools have a different understanding about discipline and its enforcement. The clash of cultures confuses the students and makes behavior-management difficult, and it undermines their efforts in creating their distinct school cultures. The principals agree that at times it feels chaotic and much energy is spent trying to keep a semblance of order. The principals agree that having their own space would reduce student behavioral problems.

The issue of space, whether it's for the individual schools or shared, is a contentious one. Shared spaces continue to challenge the council's creativity in addressing supervision and monitoring of students' behavior. The principals explained the complexity of the problem: Multiple schools use the shared facilities during the day; traffic to and from the shared facilities (i.e., gyms, library, cafeteria, auditorium, laboratories) can get chaotic; and the shortage of personnel to supervise students in multiple areas, including entrances and scanning stations, has made the task more difficult.

The principals who have schools around these shared facilities experience a greater disruption to their instructional programs than other schools in the building and are constantly challenged by discipline problems. Although students may have a legitimate reason for being in the shared space, the principals indicated that some students are easily tempted to take advantage of the opportunity to cut classes or meet friends.

It is also extremely difficult to identify which school the students belong to unless they are wearing a uniform. Although both campuses expressed their frustration with student discipline around shared spaces, there didn't seem to be a policy or agreement on how to address or alleviate the problem, for example, the library will be closed during passing or a special library pass must be used or school personnel should report to the gym areas when their students have physical education.

Despite the ongoing problems with shared space, none of the principals complained of being disrespected by students from the other schools. The principals have been able to hold students accountable for their conduct toward staff and administration of the entire campus. For now the consensus is that when students are walking through another school's space they will respect the rules.

There is a general consensus among the principals regarding expectations for students' behavior in the building: respect for people and property, tolerance, and engagement in schoolwork. However, the principals indicated that enforcing a campus-wide policy is difficult even when they've agreed to it. The problem lies in the details: identifying infractions and consequences. Whereas some principals believe in addressing the small problems (i.e., wearing hats in class or cutting class) as a preventative measure, others will focus on the bigger issues (i.e., gang fights or group violence).

Despite these differences, the principals agree that it is not the biggest problem the council faces but rather the lack of communication between and among them regarding discipline. The principals have agreed, for the most part, that fighting should result in a suspension; the conflict lies in the number of days. Although the principals believe that ultimately the principal of the school has the final say in determining consequences, they prefer that everyone abide by the campus agreement.

The unwritten agreement is that any student caught fighting gets a suspension; however, not all members of the Principals' Council always adhere to agreement. Whereas one principal may abide by the agreement, another may feel otherwise, creating discord among some of the council members. "So it creates a source of contention between you and I because that's the policy we created together. But at the end of the day, it's you who can make the decision. I can't force you to change that," explained Dr. Alvarado.

The principals understand and respect the final say of a principal in determining the consequence of an offense. Since the principal is privy to confidential information on his or her student, he should have the final say on the outcome of an investigation. However, when it comes to interschool conflicts, many of the council members believe that all the principals involved should communicate the rationale for deviating from the campus policy.

> And on the day or the week of the incident, if there is a fight, Principal A decides not to suspend and Principal B decides to suspend. I believe at that moment there should be some high level of accountability. . . . If we realize that, you know, as a consensus, this child should be suspended, I think it has to go beyond just those two parties. It has to be brought to the cabinet [council], be brought to the group. And, say, you know, "For these reasons, student A should be suspended. And we are holding you accountable." (Dr. Alvarado)

At times the disposition of a case hinges on the negotiations of the principals.

> Can we talk about it? Can we meet somewhere in the middle? So let's do it one day [student A] and one day [student B] because we don't want to treat them differently. (Mr. Messiah)

Another major factor that impacts the decision on what disciplinary actions to impose is incident reporting. "A lot of principals don't want level five [highest level of severity in NYCDOE] infractions on their school because it's all collected down at central," indicated Mr. Girgenti. All principals are required to enter information on all incidents that occur in their schools. Since this system depends on the schools for its information, some incidents may not get reported, especially those that are considered severe enough to warrant a suspension.

Many principals feel the pressure of keeping the reporting numbers low. Principal and superintendent suspensions are public information; parents review the data. "And when parents see that, they say, well, this is not a place I want to send my kids. . . . They want to attract good kids, and I don't blame them," explained Mr. Girgenti. One principal reflected on this issue: "And I think a lot of things are covered up to save face, to protect egos, and not really thinking about how to protect the campus."

For other principals, the decision to suspend is clear-cut and they are less intimidated by the collection of the data. Dr. Cruz explained his perspective on suspensions:

> In my case, there's zero tolerance for that sort of thing [fighting]. So I will give them five days. If my records were really checked, I probably have more suspensions than anybody else. But there's a reason for it, and the kids get it. I like to think so. I don't even know if I have more than I should, less than I should—I don't know what it is. All I know is that if it happens, it happens. You get it, and that's it.

The fact that not all schools follow campus policies presents a challenge to the schools that do enforce them. Commenting on the schools' discipline policies, Dr. Alvarado said, "From my end, I feel like out of the five schools, maybe two of us, maybe one of them, is really on top of the discipline." Some schools are just "running amuck." Mr. Girgenti stated, "So it makes it very difficult for certain schools to enforce certain rules when another school, out in the open, does what they want." He elaborated on why some schools feel they can openly disregard campus policies:

> Well, we were an Impact Building at one time. And we all followed the rules because [central administration] was looking at us. But now, [central administration] is not looking at us, so now the rules, it doesn't matter. They just—we do what we want here, kind of thing.

The majority of the principals believe that deviation from the campus policy should be an exception and not a norm and that they should be held accountable to the council for their decisions. The lack of accountability to the council by some members regarding their students' behavior has created some tension among the members of the council. Whereas one principal may be a strict enforcer of discipline policies, another may have a more relaxed approach to students' behavior. This difference becomes a "quality of life" issue on the campus and it's experienced by both campuses.

The intent of the campus policy seems to be at odds with the principals' understanding and commitment on discipline. It would seem that the original intent was for the policy to ensure a cohesive and unified approach to discipline enforcement. As one principal stated, "It looks good on paper." This may have been necessary to appease central administration during the Impact years when there were frequent walk-throughs by central administration and NYPD personnel and data were continuously gathered and monitored.

Central administration's demand for a unified discipline policy was an essential component of the Impact initiative. The Principals' Councils were accountable for incidents and deviations from the campus policies. However, once the campuses were removed from Impact, the need for the policy no longer existed. Central administration's "eye" was the only thing that forced the councils to give the "perception" that they were working together.

Since the councils understood that unresolved differences among the principals could result in central administration's intervention and potential unsatisfactory rating, they continued the perception of a unified campus policy despite the differences in enforcement. The council knew that keeping the infraction numbers low was sufficient to "stay off the radar" and continue to do whatever they wanted. However, this understanding meant that they did not have to work toward a collective commitment to campus life. In fact it encouraged an autonomous perspective that many principals embraced.

Central administration's mandate for a unified campus-wide discipline policy may have caused more conflict than intended as well as go against its own philosophy on small schools' autonomy and individuality. The concept of a unified discipline policy may have to be reframed from the standardized "one-size-fits-all" approach advocated by central administration during the Impact years. However, that does not exclude the need for a campus-wide discipline policy.

Interschool conflicts can get very dangerous. They have an unpredictable way of growing out of control. If left unattended, conflicts can grow to encompass the entire campus, causing violent fights and riotous conditions such as the one that the Cuomo Campus experienced. Unfortunately, once it reaches that level, containing it will take time and effort and additional external resources. Therefore it is imperative that there is an agreement on how to address interschool conflicts.

A unified campus-wide discipline code sends a strong message that the principals take interschool conflicts seriously. On the other hand, even interschool conflicts should be differentiated. There is a difference between your average student fight and a fight that can turn into group violence. The former can be addressed by the individual school but the latter should be addressed collectively.

SHARED SPACE AND INSTRUCTIONAL PROGRAMS

The instructional programs, or the thematic structures, of the schools have not been a source of contention among the principals. The principals reported that they understand and appreciate the uniqueness of the schools located within the campus. There is collegial respect from the council members for the vision and the work of the principals.

Some shared spaces did pose a challenge for the schools' instructional programs, specifically the use of gyms and the cafeteria and, on some campuses, the science labs. The use of these spaces required the collaboration of the principals. With only one cafeteria, someone was having lunch right after breakfast and someone was having it at the end of the day. With limited gym space, meeting the state and city requirements was difficult. The use of these spaces by multiple schools meant that the principals had to agree on a schedule.

And yet how to do so equitably was an issue. In the case of sharing space, the simplest way to schedule its use would be for everyone to be on one bell schedule. However, some principals argued that following the traditional "forty-five-minute-factory-like" schedule of the large school goes against the educational philosophy of small schools of creating a more personalized learning environment. It also limited how they schedule their instructional time.

There are ways around this issue if the principals are not afraid of a "messy" process unlike the predictability and standardization of the traditional forty-five-minute schedule. For example, the principals can decide to use one campus bell schedule as a starting point. They then can create their school schedule from that point. The common schedule allows for the scheduling of shared spaces.

If school A has lunch during the campus-scheduled seventh period then the principal knows that he has to stay within that allotted time, whatever that allotted time is (i.e., thirty or forty-five or even sixty minutes). So, if his school schedule is based on a sixty-minute period but the campus is based on a forty-five-minute period then the principal needs to figure out where the students will go for the additional fifteen minutes. Or he can leave his lunch period at forty-five minutes and work backward or forward in sixty-minute increments.

The same type of planning is needed for the use of gyms. It does get a bit more complicated because the lunch periods need to be considered. The complexity of the program increases with space limitation and teacher programs. In addition, teachers' contractual time will dictate how many periods they can teach in arrow or in a day. No principal wants to hire a physical education (PE) teacher that can only teach two periods because of space availability.

Some campuses have become very creative with the problem posed by the limitation of gym space and have established a "shared PE department" where the teachers teach all students regardless of the school they go to. Of course there are pros and cons to this situation such as who is in charge of supervision of a shared PE department or who handles disciplinary issues; however, that can easily be resolved among the principals.

Whether it's a fixed schedule or block schedules, the council is only limited by its creativity and flexibility. The predictability of a standard schedule gives teachers and administrators a sense of stability. This sense of stability may be a greater challenge than the use of space by multiple schools. The principals need to decide how much they can push their school without causing chaos or too much unpredictability.

Despite their differences, all of the principals believe that schools can coexist in the same building. "We're not up against each other. Everybody does their thing," stated Dr. Cruz. Mr. Girgenti agreed, 'I think it can coexist. But shared space has to always be considered." Dr. Alvarado argued that flexibility is important to the process:

> But you have to be willing to bend and realize that, you know, whether you're the one who, you know, always has the reins tightly gripped, or whether you're the one that is ready to, you know, have a rock concert with your kids, there are benefits to both sides. . . . I think everyone, every school, has a strength. And I think if we're able to tap into it, it could be a very healthy and fruitful community.

TROUBLE WITH THE LAW

The biggest challenge that underperforming large schools had was violence and disorderly conduct by students. The phaseout of the large schools was closely monitored by NYPD. The allotment of SSAs was increased in each of the large schools, and members of a new School Safety Task Force were assigned to Impact Schools.

For the next four years, the phase-out period, the principals struggled with the dichotomous views on safety. Principals believed that a safe environment was "warm and caring," conducive to learning, while the Safety Agents believed in a zero-tolerance policy for offenses, with immediate disciplinary action. Regardless of the mutual feeling among principals, the reality was that NYPD's SSA division was there to stay and the council needed to figure out how to make it work.

Both the Cuomo and the Marin Campuses continue to be scanning schools despite their restructuring, and they require a large assignment of agents. Regardless of negative perceptions of scanning, most principals on the campuses seem to want to change that situation. There is an underlying belief that "it is better to be safe than sorry." Ms. DeGioulis reflects on this:

> I used to, in the very beginning, when we started at [Cuomo Campus], I used to loathe the whole scanning process. I felt that we were treated as cattle when we got in. The same thing, like when you travel at the airport; it is very degrading. But then you also come to understand that times have changed and you see that to some degree it helps secure the safety or give us a sense of safety that we should have. So whereas in the beginning I didn't want scanning, now, I wouldn't do without scanning.

The campuses struggle with the idea of scanning, especially when speaking with parents and recruiting potential students. "The perception is, wow, look at all these cops here, this must be a bad school," commented Mr. Girgenti. However, since scanning is not an unusual practice anymore, the principals are able to reframe the conversation. "But it's a way of life now," said one principal. Most of the large schools in the city have scanning, especially those that were restructured into campuses. He said that most parents "believe that it makes their students safer that weapons don't come into the building." "We're here with your children, your babies," Dr. Alvarado explains to parents. In the end, "I'd rather be safe than sorry." Not all the principals share the same beliefs on scanning.

One principal commented on some of the council members' belief: "I could tell you that that's the belief of one of the principals in this school, at least, maybe two. They would like to remove scanning entirely." Dr. Cruz believes that the schools need to be treated as institutions of learning. Although he did not state that all security measures should be removed, he did issue a challenge to the status quo:

> I think we could spend—I would challenge the system to allow us to spend a week without them. Without scanning, without officers—you know maybe nearby, and we could call them, God forbid. But I really think that, you know, the kids would do better.

The problem with scanning is not the process itself, but rather the agents. "I have to tell you, the problem with the students is the security agents," stated Mr. Girgenti. A firm believer that the morning entrance will set the tone for the rest of the day, he argues that the last thing that should be done is to "yell at the kids." It is important that students are "greeted with warmth, with sincerity, with care," a sentiment that is shared by all the principals. They all expressed concern about the scanning process, especially in the morning. Mr. Girgenti expressed his displeasure at the procedures the SSA's employ:

> You know the CPR on the police code, "courtesy, professionalism and respect"? It doesn't exist in 99 percent of them. They're not welcoming; they're not happy in the morning. And my kids especially have short fuses and they let them know. And I have a problem literally every week with somebody coming through scanning. Even in the rain they were making the kids take their boots off. We had a big thing about that. What, they're going to step on the wet floor in there? If you hand-wand them, you know, there are techniques. If they ring differently in one boot to the other, then you know there may be something in there. And they could do one foot at a time. Take your foot out of one and then put it back in and then do the next. They were making them take their shoes off going through scanning. It was ridiculous.

The Marin Campus has two schools with a large number of limited-English-speaking students, many who are newcomers to the country. These students' experiences with SSAs have, at times, been antagonistic, making adjustment to school difficult. Mr. Lipchitz described some of the SSA's disposition toward the ESL students:

> I think that they are picked on more, but I don't think School Safety realizes it, even though they've been told. Because they say things like, "Take off your hat!" or "Do this!" and the student doesn't respond. . . . They don't understand what you're saying. They don't speak English. "Well, they better learn!"

Dr. Cruz has had similar experiences with morning scanning:

> And your parent just woke you up and gave you breakfast, or sent you to school early to have breakfast. So you go to school and the first thing you do is you have an SSA yelling at you and screaming at you, and if not, worse. And we've tried to tell them, "Look, these kids that are here the earliest are the kids that want to be in school, so be friendly with them. You should always be warm to them, if you can say "good morning" to at least get them through scanning as quickly as possible without making their lives impossible because you have some sort of frustration that's not their fault.

The relationship between SSAs and school staff is contentious and will elicit an emotional response from the principals when asked about it. All the principals stated that it has been a work in progress. They acknowledge that there are some good SSAs that work well with students but many lack the skills to be in a school building. Dr. Alvarado recalled her early experience with the SSAs:

> At the beginning when we first got here, there were some major issues in terms of being on the same page, because I found that a lot of the agents wanted to be, just be people who berated kids and berated adults or people who wanted to just be friends. So you would walk with the kids; you would walk by and you would hear agents having inappropriate conversations with students, using foul language, using sexual conversation, just things that were inappropriate. And for me, I found that we had to do something about it. So the relationship has been very much strained between School Safety and myself. And I'm going to say, with other schools as well—but when it comes to that relationship, I very much have a no-tolerance policy.

It has been a balancing act: reporting of incidents with SSA and supporting them. "It's a double-edged sword, because you don't want them to be on the wrong side, because you need them to respond and help in case you need them," explained Dr. Cruz. Because principals don't have the authority to discipline SSA, the reporting system becomes cumbersome. Dr. Alvarado explained how this undermines the principal's authority and impacts school discipline:

> I think a lot of things changed when the NYPD became accountable for school safety. But I don't believe that the Department of Education should have been totally removed from the picture. I think that principals should have a say in disciplining SSAs. I think that principals should have a say in who stays and who goes.

The principals felt that their lack of authority over the SSA caused undue conflict with them. The SSAs know that the principals have no jurisdiction over them and, therefore, have no authority to tell them what to do. And the agents were quick to point out this detail to the principals. The "you can't tell me what to do" has been heard by the principals on the campus at one time or the other. Dr. Alvarado stated that she even had one female agent tell her, "Well, I'm grown. You can't tell me what to do."

For some SSA the fact that principals had no jurisdiction over them was enough reason to push the envelope regarding their authority. In situations like this, principals engaged in letter writing, documenting incidents and unprofessional conduct of the agents. It was a lengthy bureaucratic process for the agents to be disciplined, without any guarantees that the SSA would be disciplined.

The principals were uncannily unanimous in their beliefs regarding SSAs: Most lack the proper training to work with students or in schools. All of the principals have observed some SSAs repeatedly engaging in unprofessional behaviors (e.g., cursing, conversations with students laced with sexual innuendos, confiscating items illegally and not returning them, etc.). The principals have also witnessed agents' negative dispositions toward their students (e.g., yelling, cursing, degrading comments, etc.).

The different approach to student behavior is a source of contention between the principals and the agents. The role of the SSAs (post-NYPD) as police officers has caused conflict with many principals who believe that the schools should be a place of learning and not one where youth offenses are criminalized. The principals on the campus argued that some agents were overzealous in their efforts to confiscate "contraband" (i.e., phones and iPods) resulting in students becoming angry and insubordinate. Many times the situation became hostile enough to cause the arrest of the student or the issuance of a summons.

Mr. Lipchitz has had his share of experiences with SSAs and is the most vocal about their disposition. He indicated that the unnecessary use of force is his biggest concern with the agents:

> And the SSA sees them [students] with the phone, runs after them and starts yelling at them, and the kid says, "I'm going to see --." And it becomes this huge, huge thing where the kid is on the ground in handcuffs . . . just going to see his counselor with a phone. That was after they came and said phones are not weapons.

The issuance of a summons or even the arrest of a student for insubordination to a SSA was troubling for the principals at many levels. A large percentage of students at both campuses have had multiple encounters with police officers, most of them unpleasant. Other students have been incarcerated before and the negative encounters with a SSA add to the animosity between them.

For the principals, the issuance of summons and arrest created another layer of problems, namely, the monitoring of incidents by central administration. Every summons issued or arrest made by an agent was recorded by the NYPD and compared to what the school was reporting. This was particularly troubling in a school where the principal was reluctant to report incidents. During the Impact years, a discrepancy in the numbers of incidents reported by NYPD and DOE was followed by a visit from central administration to the campus, demanding an explanation.

However, the principals understood that they risked not getting the support from the agents if they perceived the principals were setting them up to be disciplined. The principals indicated there was a fine line when dealing with the agents: Push too hard and the agents won't respond when needed or don't push hard enough and the agents continue to engage in unprofessional conduct.

Notwithstanding the challenges with SSAs, the principals agreed that the majority of the agents are good and well-intentioned individuals but lack the necessary training to work with students. For now, the conversation revolves around how to make the school feel warm and welcoming, regardless of the problems with some SSAs or the scanning process.

The principals agreed that there had been some improvement in their relationship with the SSAs. They believe that the council's articulation of expectations for SSA behaviors, and consistently enforcing those expectations in addition to the small schools' discipline policies, have been instrumental in strengthening the partnership. Nevertheless, it continues to be a work in progress, with the principals ever vigilant of the interactions between their students and the agents.

The Impact years were extremely difficult for everyone. The mandate to reduce violence and bring order to the schools created stressful conditions for administrators and law enforcement alike, but it also added fuel to an already strained relationship. Principals felt that their work of creating a "safe and personalized learning environment" was being undermined by the heavy presence of agents that patrolled the halls with intent of "crackin' down" on violators.

On the other hand, the agents and officers felt that educators challenged their authority in their pursuit to bring order. The goals were not so different, whatever the means were, and that created the conflict. It took several years before the council and the SSA division was able to find—if not happy—a workable medium.

Campuses that developed post-Impact years find that the relationship with the SSAs and NYPD is better. For one thing, they don't have to contend with the pressures of the Impact initiative or its public exposure. Secondly, there has been a greater effort made to train agents to work in schools. Campuses that were created without the Impact stigma did not experience the same level of chaos as the ones that were subjected to it. However they still had to develop and maintain a positive relationship with the School Safety Division.

This task was made easier when the roles were better defined and expectations were made clearer. The roles of the principal and the agent are not interchangeable. An agent can't tell a principal to suspend a student any more than a principal can tell an agent to arrest a child. An agent can't assign a staff member to a post any more that a principal can tell an agent to patrol. However, when the principals and the agents work collaboratively, the conversation revolves around to how to effectively use the resources to create and maintain a safe environment.

For the most part, school leaders and law enforcement officers want to work together to create safe learning environments. And it usually works well. The impact of their presence is even greater when they work with the individual students. More importantly, the benefit and the rewards of such a relationship is far reaching. When youth officers establish a positive relationship with students in a safe environment like a school it translates to a better relationship on the streets.

A strong partnership with law enforcement is important not just to build positive community relationships but also for the safety of students. Crisis is a reality that all schools contend with, whether it's a violent incident or an accident. There must be a protocol for initiating a response plan and maintaining contact with the police. Most districts have established those protocols. However, with multiple principals in a campus it can get confusing if the lines of communications are not clear. Everyone needs to know what principal is in charge at any given time. There is no room for error.

CONCLUSION

The reality of campus life calls for creativity, ingenuity, and flexibility. The traditional way of doing things may not work and the simplest way may not meet the needs of all. Even retrofitting old buildings to accommodate the multiple schools may not meet the needs of the individual programs. One public address (PA) system may work for one school's schedule but may not meet the needs of another. Or even if the PA system could accommodate the schedule of multiple schools, it would still create havoc with the shared-space schedule.

Budgetary concerns are another reality that campus principals need to contend with every year. Funding personnel and enrichment programs that can only be done on a campus-wide basis requires the contribution of all schools, regardless of their students' participation. Yet, not all the schools may be able to contribute the same amount. The principals need to find an equitable solution to this problem.

And if managing space and money were not sufficient to test the skills of the principals, they must deal with thousands of students in the building. Many of the large-school buildings can handle between one thousand and three thousand students. With so many students in a building, discipline is another reality of campus life. However, discipline can be interpreted differently depending on the culture of the school. How to live and work with those differences is yet another challenge for the principals.

Reconciling these realities with the multiple needs of the schools stretches the imagination of the council. Solving these problems will take reframing problems, negotiation, and compromise. Negotiation takes time and compromise requires consensus. But in the end it will yield positive results. Living on a dysfunctional campus should not be an option when there are many experienced and knowledgeable school leaders on it.

Chapter 5

Where's the Boss? The Role of Central Administration

Mayor Bloomberg was on a mission. He gained control of the schools and changed the Board of Education into the Department of Education by replacing an elected board with a virtually powerless panel (Panel on Education). He eliminated thirty-two community school boards and replaced them with ten school regions. And this was just the beginning.

In its zeal to reform the schools in the city, the administration took on multiple reform efforts, some simultaneously and others consecutively. However, the pace left little time for evaluation, and as a result there were constant changes being made. Reforms were adopted, adapted, and then modified—only to be modified again. This constant flux created a stressful environment for the schools.

The current administration knew that systemic changes were needed if they were going to make any significant impact on student achievement. They also understood that the current bureaucratic system was going to be an impediment to that process. Reforms needed to be done on a large scale and quickly. Changing the landscape of schools was going to be huge undertaking. Doing this while restructuring central administration was an even greater task.

Closing a school, opening a school, and building a council are distinct and complex undertakings requiring specific sets of skills and commitment. Taking on these challenges simultaneously in the context of the Impact status may be explained by central administration's underestimation of the challenge or ignorance of the complexity of the work involved or both. Regardless of central's understanding or lack thereof, the constant changes created a lot of uncertainty as they tried to develop their schools. Their effort was also hampered by central's lack of support structures for campus management.

The principals from both the Cuomo and the Marin Campus expressed how exasperating it was to try and get the help they needed. And not just for campus-management issues. There were support services and guidance they needed to operate their schools. However, the constant changes made operational and compliance issues very difficult to manage. Finding the right person to help them was like looking for a needle in the haystack. Couple this with trying to develop a council that collectively would manage a campus was extremely stressful for the principals.

Nevertheless, both campuses grappled with the decision-making process; everything from a shared-campus discipline policy, to the use of shared space, to agreeing on budget allocations was a struggle. This task would have been less stressful if central administration had created systems and structures to support the Principals' Council.

Unfortunately, even central administration would have had difficulty providing support since they had not developed the human capacity to help the council and were too busy experimenting with school and district governance. The lack of structures and human capacity had a profound and long-lasting effect on the council's development. The role of central administration cannot be overlooked in campus formation and especially not in council development. The Principals' Council on both campuses attests to that fact.

CONSTANT FLUX

The small-school principals were frustrated with central administration's instability, which caused them to struggle with day-to-day operations in addition to campus management:

> What happens is there were so many evolving changes in between, simultaneously. . . . I mean, 2003, when we opened, is when the mayor took over, the regions [were created] there were no more districts. That was a big change. And then, there were no more regions. And then, there was no more this. And then, there were networks. And then there were networks plus the other thing.
>
> Every year, each of those entities—you know, Special Ed, security, budget, you know, everything that is needed to run a school, and all the experts were dispersed and gone and creating little entities. And then, we're here, this small school, you know, trying to keep up. And who do we call? We'll call this one. Who do we call? Call that one . . . "Oh, I'm not in charge anymore. You got to call that one." "Oh no, that's not me. I don't do that anymore. It's this one." You know, call over here. . . . And even now, we all have different networks. And each of them, you know, wants to support their schools. And they all do it in a different way. And nobody knows what's what! (Dr. Cruz)

A network of individuals serve each school on the campus. This clustering of schools was the fifth restructuring of school operations by central administration since 2003. Under the current central administration organizational structure, networks provided the first line of support to schools. The networks provided most of the instructional services that traditional school district staff would have provided in addition to some operational support such as budgeting and human resources.

Noninstructional services, such as facilities, have been centralized. Each school, not the campus, selects a network that they want to be affiliated with, so that technically every school on the campus can have a different network providing services. This context becomes very important when trying to understand the complexity of campus decision making. Any disagreement that requires a network intervention is problematic because it will be ineffective at best and pointless, complained Mr. Messiah:

> And the reason for that is each school is in a different SSO [school support organization], PSO [partnership school organization], whatever network support, right. So that means that if we have an issue, we are supposed to go to that but they have no ties into budget. They don't have the resources for operations—or anything else. So there's a problem if you have four and five different people come to the table with us . . . arguing the same problem.
>
> "Oh, reach your [network]. Network has no answers. The SSO that they're working in has no answer. Like, my person has no answers with facilities; none whatsoever. Her job is instruction, goals, data analysis, and let me see what I can do. That's it.

The intent of the networks may have been to reduce the layers of bureaucracy for the schools; however, this too became an obstacle. The networks had no real power. They were just intermediaries. The networks still had to go through central administration to get approval for anything dealing with operations. In essence, the schools were still dependent on central, they just couldn't go to them directly.

During the early stages of the reform, central administration created an office to support the ever-expanding portfolio of schools. However, the speed and scale of school development—more than forty large schools closed during the 2002–2009 time period, creating campuses that total over two hundred schools—limited central's capacity to engage with the schools.

Even the creation of the Department of School Governance, responsible for supporting campus governance, could not keep up with the demand of campus development, so much so that few principals knew of its role. Mr. Girgenti commented, "I'm not even sure what they are. . . . I know there is a division in the Department of Ed for campus support. I honestly don't know much about it. So I guess it has not been communicated to us well enough."

The limited role of the Department of School Governance, coupled with the constant change at central administration, made it very difficult to reach out for help. More importantly, asking for help was not encouraged. In fact, it was discouraged:

> And believe me when I say to you that the cliché says, "We don't air our dirty laundry outside this room." That's part of the problem and they all believe in that. And that's why they won't seek other people's help, because they don't want to think anybody out there thinks that they're having a problem. Because you know that if a campus complains that they need help or support, it gets to the hierarchy. And they look down, "You guys, you need to work this out. I don't need to hear this," that kind of thing. So they feel that pressure of not seeking help because of the way it's structured. And I think that would make a lot of principals reluctant to ask for support. (Mr. Girgenti)

The situation was tenuous with central's threat to decrease the number of points a principal can receive by the superintendent in their Principal's Performance Review (PPR) and potentially reduce their rating.

> We were told this year, right, as campus principals, that if the superintendent has to intervene, it's a reduction in your PPR points. How stupid is that? You know, they expect us, if a teacher has a problem, to come to the supervisor and deal with it. If the assistant principals have a problem, take it to the principal. But, if the principals have a problem, we cannot go to anybody. We have to deal with it. (Mr. Messiah)

The principal was referring to the 2009 Campus Policy Memo (seven years after the first large-school closing was announced) issued by central administration, explaining the protocols for dealing with unresolved issues on the campuses and delineating the procedure for resolving campus-wide disputes. According to central administration, the campus holds the "locus of control" over building-wide decisions and, therefore, resolutions should be made at that level.

If the campus is unable to reach an agreement, then the schools' networks are involved in the process. But as the principals have indicated, the role of the networks was limited. The schools pay the network for their services, therefore they have no authority to make any demands on a principal. As a result, the principals are less likely to reach out to their network, knowing that they are just as powerless in holding another principal accountable to the council. Hence most principals would prefer to live with the ongoing conflict than bring in central administration and get an adverse rating.

Central administration's voluntary blindness to the council's conflict is a reflection of its punitive policy of "get it done or else." Central administration will not interfere with the Principals' Council as long as the problem remains within the campus. More importantly, central administration has effectively held itself "safe-harmless" from the accountability process because it is easier to blame the council for not negotiating in good faith than assist the council.

The principals are not oblivious to this policy and the resulting consequences. And despite the challenges of campus life and the fragile relationship among the members of the council, they were not willing to articulate them in an environment where dialogue and problem solving is not encouraged. As a result, the principals continue to live with unresolved issue.

Although both campuses were eventually established and the Impact status removed, the councils are at different points of development. This is evident in the decision-making process of the principals and the Principals' Council. Whereas some principals will be cognizant of the impact their decisions have on the campus, others will not hesitate to implement a new program or schedule. Whereas one campus has norms for consensus, the other struggles to establish norms.

WHO'S IN CHARGE?

The multiple reforms and changes in central administration created an unstable environment for the new small schools to operate in. The role of the superintendent had changed. The authority of the network was limited. The division responsible for campus management was overwhelmed. Autonomy for principals was advocated to the point of relinquishment of supervision by central administration. This allowed central administration to hold itself "safe-harmless" from any consequences resulting from the principals' mistakes.

However, many of the principals believed that central administration should have taken a more active role in campus development, especially with the Principals' Council, not in a dictatorial way but more of a facilitating manner.

> I think it may have been more effective for campus schools, because, again, you have different leadership styles here. You have a level of autonomy that people may be able to handle as a school principal. But as one of the many other school principals in the building, there has to be, again, someone who is able to come in and see whether or not things are working. And not just say, "Well, you're adults. You have to make it work." But, you know, sometimes people still need that guiding hand. So, I believe that the district [administration] could have been the guiding hand that the campuses would have benefited from. (Dr. Alvarado)

Most of the experienced administrators believed that the sheer number of new and inexperienced principals during campus development necessitated the involvement of the central administration or of someone with the authority to make "executive" decisions. These experienced administrators knew that the "autonomy and empowerment" movement was creating havoc, with the council giving some principals the impression that they were not accountable for their decisions.

They were also well aware of how incapacitating the stubbornness of one member could be to the entire negotiating process. It only took the actions of one principal for everything to come to a standstill or worse.

> You know, we say we love autonomy and the empowerment. But when there comes issues of challenge, of reprimand, of discipline, you know, in order not to get to that point, I believe there should be someone who is looking in and checking, and not "gotcha" but seeing how we're growing. (Dr. Alvarado)

The principals made it a point to clarify the support they were looking for from central or the network. Most of the principals wanted to work together and work through the problems collectively. However, they also knew that some of their colleagues were having difficulty with collaborative work and reaching consensus. Campus management was new to everyone. Many hoped that central or the networks would provide the guidance that was needed to develop the Principals' Council. But they also understood that some principals—by their nature—would make it difficult.

The principals wanted to have someone to help them if they reached an impasse or if there were issues of equity that could not be resolved internally. More importantly, the principals needed to know that if another principal did not want to be accountable to the council, he or she had to be accountable to someone. And if a "reprimand or discipline" was required then it should be only for the principal creating the problem not the entire council.

The central administration's policy regarding the Principals' Council "locus of control" had the best of intentions. There is no doubt that empowerment and autonomy are critical elements for school leaders to perform at optimal levels. Micromanagement is always counterproductive and counterintuitive. Usually the best decisions are made by the people that are most impacted by the problem at hand. They understand the issues and the factors that play an important role in those issues. Having someone come in and make decisions undermines and disempowers the people impacted.

However, there is a fine line between supervision and micromanagement; the former is supporting and the latter is controlling. That's not to say that supervision is only about supporting with guidance and training. There is a difficult component to supervision: reprimand and discipline. It's the part of being a boss that most bosses dislike. Nevertheless it is an integral component to supervision.

During the Bloomberg/Klein administration, there was an "empower-autonomy-accountability" motto. Central administration's quest to empower principals gave them a reason to become lax in their supervision. Central could then focus on implementing more reforms. Unfortunately when council dysfunction became a problem they imposed stiff penalties instead of providing supervision and support. The policy of "getting done or else" only accomplished one thing for councils: hiding the problem from central and living with dysfunction.

The principals in the council referred to the fact that there wasn't a "boss." The networks were not bosses since the schools paid for their services. The superintendent's role was limited; in fact, they rarely visited schools during the Bloomberg/Klein administration although this has recently changed, again. Despite the fact that the principals enjoy their autonomy, they understood its drawbacks and limitations, especially within the council.

BUILDING CAPACITY

There was a rapid increase in campus formation during the Bloomberg/Klein administration. Schools did not need to be closed to justify the creation of a campus. The charter school movement created another reason for campus development. The current administration paved the way for charter schools to be located in public school buildings. Co-location allowed charter and public schools to share the same building.

Co-location is a creative way to provide space in underutilized schools or provide on-site services to the students and the community. In fact, many campuses today have multiple configurations: Pre-K–12, public and charter, Spec Ed schools and traditional schools, and many others. In addition, some have multiple nonprofit organizations residing in them. But it has also created some challenges that some school leaders are having difficulties addressing.

Unlike one principal making room in their school for a clinic, you now have multiple principals vying for space in the building, and these space needs were not static, adding another unknown factor to the equation. Although these buildings were being retrofitted to accept multiple residents, their design limitation made sharing an inevitable reality.

The odds of something going wrong in a campus setting increases incrementally with every leader added to the mix. Every principal and executive director is guided by the vision and mission of their school or organization and brings with them a unique perspective to the fold. But they also come with distinct personalities and skill sets. The mix of mission, personalities, and skills can create competing views on operational decisions. Although this conflict is not necessarily a bad thing it can be paralyzing if not handled appropriately.

Building collaborative-leadership capacity to handle decision making has never been more important in a school setting. It cannot be assumed that the leaders coming into the campus setting will be able to shift their thinking from an autonomous decision maker to a member of a collective that makes the decision on a campus. That's not to say that being a collaborative leader in one's school is not important or necessary.

Being able to work collaboratively with key constituents in the school provides opportunity for shared decision making and holds everyone accountable for student achievement. However, regardless of the collaborative work, the principal will always be held accountable for all decisions; it's where the "buck stops." But that is not the case in campus management. The entire council is responsible and accountable for the campus.

It is imperative that central administration vets principals for these particular traits, or at least that they have the disposition to be trained to work in a campus setting. Motivation and disposition are more important than work experience. A person who does not have the experience or the specific skill sets but is willing to learn is a lot more desirable than someone who has a lot of work experience but is unable to work collaboratively with other principals.

And there are people who do not like being part of a team. They want to make the decisions and have no problem taking the credit for the work of others. It may be difficult to believe but there are many principals that cannot work in a collaborative manner even within their own school. There may be a school for a person with this kind of disposition (maybe) but certainly not on a campus.

There has been increased pressure for districts and leadership programs to emphasize a corporate model glorifying "lone visionary" CEOs that transform organizations: turning their dysfunctional organization into an efficient and effective one; turning loss into profit; and changing public perceptions. And although there are similarities in the leadership work that CEOs and educational leaders do, there is one important difference: Principals are responsible for the academic and social development of *human beings* not cars or houses or furniture or even financial portfolios.

This key difference underscores the challenging task that principals have in their schools and their communities. There are a myriad of factors involved in educating human beings that are not under the control of the principal, from family issues to cultural differences to socioeconomic problems to political agendas, not to mention human development.

However, the greatest skill many of these successful CEO possess is their ability to see the interconnection of the world around them and what that means to their organization. In the long term, it's not about closing yourself off but branching out and forging successful ventures and partnerships. This is the vision that should be espoused by district offices. And the Principals' Council is a great place to start the conversation on collaborative leadership.

Building capacity at the campus level requires a level of expertise that is best left to professionals. Initially a third party, like a university or a well-trained and experienced consultant, should do this training. There are a few reasons for this approach. For one thing, universities have programs that are geared toward developing and coaching leaders.

These programs are facilitated in a nonthreatening way. Their aim is to build the necessary trust to engage individuals in the challenging task of building relationships and solving conflicts. Most districts are not equipped to facilitate this type of training. Training of this caliber has a long-lasting effect, as the principal explained below, and not just on their professional life.

> And it was a very intense retreat. It was at the University of Penn. So we learned—class instructions—about team dynamics, about goal setting, about doing the right thing. And then, another piece about team building was on protocols. And one of the things that they did, that's still fresh in my mind, is the 360 evaluations. You know, how your supervisor thinks about you, and how your colleagues and your subordinates think of you, and how the circle completes itself, and how true it was with several of us. (Mr. Messiah)

Secondly, the principals will approach training done by central administration with a different mind-set. Most training that is done by central is viewed as meeting a compliance issue or a mandate: how to, when to, and why to do something. That type of training or professional development is fine but it has its place and time and this is not it. Although central administration can mandate that the principals in the council work together, they cannot force collaboration. Mandated collaboration is an oxymoron. Collaboration stems from a good relationship, and that takes work.

It is also best for principals to be out of their buildings when engaging in this training. Principals are easily distracted and disturbed by staff if they are in their building. And if you add cell phones to the mix then you are sure to lose the principals' attention. Training for collaborative leadership is intense work. You have to break down misconceptions about autonomy and collaboration in order to build a working relationship based on mutual understanding and trust.

Ideally the training should be held off the campus school building. Conducting the training outside of the building allows for principals to delve into the concept of collaborative leadership. Principals will have time to reflect on their practice, probe their understandings on school leadership, and examine their strengths and weaknesses in light of their training. Principals will also need time to bond in a nonthreatening or pressured environment. Sharing meals and drinks in a collegial setting is not only relaxing but the foundation to a fruitful collaboration.

The principals of the campuses praised their initial training and the impact it had on the council, personal relationships, and school tone. One principal commented, "It was like, 'Wow. It's amazing.' . . . I mean, we went out to dinners together. We went out for drinks together. I think it was a good opening in tone."

This type of training helps build a solid foundation for establishing protocols. Creating protocols will be one of the most important tasks the principals will have to take on. And this is a lot harder than it sounds. It is difficult for multiple leaders to agree on anything right off the bat. However, most leaders understand the value of good partnership and are willing to engage in setting protocols if it builds a solid relationship and a profitable partnership.

Establishing those protocols collectively gives everyone an opportunity to engage in conversations; discuss the issues at hand; brainstorm, and ultimately reach an agreement that they can all live with. Not because it was handed down or mandated. It does not mean that everyone will get what he or she want, but he or she will be able to live with the decision.

Protocols do not have to be as formal as by laws but they should be documented in meeting minutes at a minimum and signed off on. This will ensure that all parties are part of the decision-making process and will abide by those agreements. It is important to note that all agreements are subject to change as long as it is done by consensus of the group and not at the whim of an individual. There are several reasons—such as a change in leadership or school needs—why agreements may require revisiting.

Learning to give and take is important in any relationship, including work relationships. But equity is equally important. Equity is not just about equal access; it includes equal responsibility. In the Principals' Council, all the members are equally responsible and accountable for the campus and should abide by the decisions made at the council meetings. Violation of this basic principle can have devastating effect on the council's relationships.

The initial retreat must be followed with additional support sessions. It's important for principals to bring concerns, issues, and ideas to the group and brainstorm options and solutions in a nonthreatening environment. The follow-up sessions are critical to the success of the group. If the group has not been able to develop a working relationship and understandings about their work then the initial session will have been for naught.

This was especially evident in one of the campuses where the principals participated in a retreat and had the temporary support of a coach. Dr. Alvarado lamented the results of the discontinued support.

> But that kind of died down. And people didn't—I mean people, yes, continued bickering. But they became less responsible for the campus and saw it as just a building where I have my school, but very little campus unity.

Obviously this "kumbaya" moment does not come cheap and neither will the follow-up sessions or the coach that works with the principals. However, the long-term benefits of a high-performing council outweigh the cost of such retreat-style training. A collaborative council supports each other and is able to bring onto the campus the resources that one school may not be able to do. On the other hand, a dysfunctional council can threaten the safety and security of a campus and deprive students of services. More importantly, it will sabotage the work of the small schools on the campus.

Building campus capacity starts with district-level capacity. Central administration should have individuals at their disposal that are well prepared to facilitate and coach a Principals' Council. These individuals or the team are responsible for supporting the governance of the campus Principals' Council and should not take on a supervisory role; that would belong to the superintendent. The goal of these individuals or team should be to help the council work collaboratively that dynamics may change if the boss is in the room. These individuals should be well versed in relationship building, conflict resolution and mediation, negotiation, and of course, school leadership. They should understand the complexities of school governance and campus life. There is nothing worse for a principal than working with someone who has no concept of school life or the challenges of being a principal. That is one sure way of losing the principal's interest and respect. People that work with principals need to have a healthy respect for the work they do and the challenges they encounter on a daily basis.

Providing this additional support to the council can be done internally or externally, such as creating a department responsible for school governance or through consulting. Partnering with the university or organization that provided the initial training may be an ideal way to build trust and continuity for the council. A third party may be less stressful for the principals. This may also encourage the principals to find solutions instead of having a solution be imposed by central. In addition, this support will be the council capacity to work collaboratively.

A council that is properly trained may not need the services of an outside party to reach consensus; however, there may be times when negotiations come to a standstill. It is not uncommon for negotiation to become deadlocked or break down. Having a third party may help a stalemate situation. It is important that the council receive the help it needs to break through the impasse and reach consensus. More importantly, the council should be encouraged to ask for assistance and not be punished for doing so. In the end, it's about building capacity for collaborative leadership and not mandating a solution.

THE SUPERINTENDENT

Ideally, once the Principals' Council has developed collaborative-leadership capacity, they will be able to work through the issues that arise on the campus. And if additional support is needed, then central's team can come in and mediate. Central's team or designated third party should not be the one to mandate or force an agreement. This is where the boss comes in.

The role of the superintendent in this conflict is to assess the situation and the interventions provided, evaluate the recommendations given and determine their feasibility, and in the end make a decision. The difficult part of this process is addressing the person(s) who is stalling or derailing the process. Involving the boss always complicates things. It is easy for the boss, in this case the superintendent, to make an executive decision and then walk away.

Unfortunately, the principals would be left to work through any potential antagonism remaining from a disciplinary conference. Hopefully the superintendent understands the difficult position the council could be left in and addresses the situation correctly. He or she should aim to understand why the principal(s) feel so strongly as to stall or derail a negotiation and address those concerns. One can hope that the recalcitrant principal will see the light.

It is hard to believe that an educator and leader can be so intractable as to stall or derail a negotiation done in good faith, nonetheless it happens more often than not. It could be blamed on lack of training or the inexperience of the principal. It may even be blamed on the sense of power that autonomy brings. However in the end, such inflexibility, intractability, and obstinacy has no more room in school leadership than negligence and/or incompetence.

The situation of this magnitude needs to be addressed with urgency. Failure to do so enables the principal to believe that this course of action is appropriate and acceptable. It also disempowers the council to move on with the business of managing the campus. An intractable principal fosters resentment, antagonism, and eventually hostility in the council. There will be a climate of distrust among the principals. Negotiation will be attempted but will fail. Equity will be fought for but never achieved. And in the end, a dysfunctional council will never be able to achieve its potential.

The superintendent needs to get the principals back on track with the business of managing the campus and running their schools. Otherwise he/she will be spending a lot of time resolving campus problems. The superintendent should be clear about his/her expectations for council collaboration and hold them accountable without micromanaging them. And without giving ultimatums of "get it done or else." It is a balancing act for the superintendent.

It is important for the council to feel supported by the superintendent. The council members should believe that they could go to the superintendent and receive guidance on how to address a problem. The superintendent should also be able to determine if it's one member that needs addressing or if the entire council needs further training. The difficult part for the superintendent is to provide this support without showing bias or preference for any one principal.

CONCLUSION

The one area where all the principals agreed they needed support and guidance was with the work of the Principals' Council. The majority of the members understood and accepted their role in managing the campus. They understood the need for collaboration among the principals, and for the most part, the principals were willing to compromise. Unfortunately, this was not the case with all the principals.

It may be possible to rationalize a principal's inability to collaborate as inexperience or his/her misunderstanding of autonomy. It may even be possible to explain a principal's unwillingness to collaborate as the "market-competition" philosophy advocated by the administration that created such high levels of stress to meet accountability benchmarks.

However, the reality of the situation is that some of the principals' refusal to engage in collaborative work was due to the "hands-off" approach from central administration. This approach enabled the principals to cling to their autonomy at the expense of the campus collective. It also allowed the central administration to hold itself "safe-harmless" of any potential negative consequence resulting from a principal's decision.

The entire Bloomberg/Klein administration was marked by an overemphasis on autonomy to the point of supervisory exclusion. The networks had no supervisory role. The superintendents had no instructional role. That left the principals to their own devices. As long as the schools received a good grade it did not matter what the principals did. For most principals this was not a problem until multiple principals were placed in one building.

Regrettably, the principals on a campus were not equipped to handle the ensuing conflicts caused by the failure to reach consensus. Campus management became difficult. Left on their own, many Principals' Councils lived with their dysfunction. They knew that any potential exposure to the central administration could lead to unsatisfactory ratings for the council members.

The failure of central administration to train and support the principals led to many dysfunctional campuses. It did not train all the principals in the council in the collaborative skills necessary to reach consensus. Central administration also failed to provide guidance and support in campus management and denied the principals the supervisory support of a superintendent.

As with any new reform it is important to create systems that will ensure its success and outlive the administration implementing them. Building capacity at the campus level as well as at central administration will significantly reduce the potential for dysfunctional campuses by increasing the effectiveness of the Principals' Council. Further, a stable and supporting superintendent will provide the principals with a sense of security during the transition.

Conclusion

Creating a Better Transitioning Plan

Two opposing emotions enveloped the phase-out schools: the joy of new beginnings and the anger of the end. At the same time, the new Impact Schools initiative was being rolled out, imposing a punitive and order-maintenance policing on the campuses. Dozens of SSAs, police officers, and central administration personnel invaded the large buildings with a zero-tolerance approach to disorder. Understanding the context in which the phaseout occurred provides an additional dimension to the drama that unfolded on these two campuses.

The founding principals on the campuses were excited to start their new school; all were winners in the grueling competition for new-schools proposals. Hours of planning, sweat, and tears went into creating the school they were about to open. They designed their own theme-based curriculum; hired staff that shared similar understandings on how students learn best; and recruited students that were interested in attending their theme-based school. Not even the placement of their school in a large school viewed as failing and unsafe curbed their enthusiasm. They had no doubt that it would work.

The large school, on the other hand, was experiencing a totally different situation. These schools suffered from a myriad of problems symptomatic of neglect: high truancy, low graduation rates, and violence. Many of these schools suffered from physical neglect and decay. Working with a challenging population under the most severe conditions was not conducive to good teaching or learning. When the schools were declared Impact, many of the teachers were under the impression that they would finally receive the support they needed to help the students achieve academically. However, that would not be the case.

Superimpose phase-out and start-up scenarios, and an unreceptive environment was inevitable. The campus principals called it "messy" and "hostile."

The buildings were still overcrowded. Although the small schools lived to tell the story, it was four years of turmoil and frustrations. The principals contended that they constantly had to defend their schools from the negative public perception of the large school and its status as underperforming and violent.

The principals acknowledged that establishing their schools those first few years was extremely challenging. There was constant jostling for space as it was carved out in the building, and getting six principals to agree to anything was nearly impossible. Even scheduling fire drills became an exercise in futility. Nevertheless, in 2011, three years after the last cohort of the large schools graduated, the buildings were no longer considered violent, building capacity was under control, and the halls were calmer. And the Impact status was lifted.

NOT SO EASY

The founding school principals agreed that the phase-out process was difficult for both the small schools and the large school. They were equally challenged in establishing the Principals' Council. The first three years, the principals dealt with the day-to-day challenges of running a school in addition to experiencing relocation pains as space was carved out through the construction process. Worrying about the campus was not a priority.

The closing-school principal made most of the decisions affecting the campus those first few years. Everything from writing the safety plan to scheduling fire drills, sorting mail to scheduling the use of shared spaces, and paying for the bulk of shared campus expenses was handled by the closing-school principal. As the schools reached a full complement of grades and the phaseout was in its final stages, the Principals' Council began to take on more campus responsibilities.

The Principals' Council was created to ensure that all principals had equal rights and responsibilities in the decision-making process regarding issues that impacted the campus. The theory behind this concept is that a campus that is well managed creates opportunities and conditions for success. Implied in this statement is the understanding that there is, or must be, a strong working relationship among the members of the council and that its members will abide by its decisions.

The decisions made by the principals, individually and collectively, ultimately impact the campus. Therefore the results of those decisions, good or bad, will depend on the strength of the relationship among the principals. However, a partnership that is forged in the midst of turmoil may not result in the ideal relationship. For the campus principals in the phase-out schools, closing a large, underperforming, and violent school, and starting new small schools, was not conducive to creating a strong and cohesive council.

A deeper look into the areas that cause the most disruptions on the campus shows that they stemmed from the council itself. The inability to reach consensus on campus-wide discipline issues, recurring problems with space and budgets, and lack of transparency in decision making has stifled the growth of the council. Many of the principals believe that there is a lack of accountability to the council and have expressed their frustrations with their inability to hold their colleagues responsible for stated and agreed decisions.

Negotiations and resolution of campus disputes are continuing challenges related primarily to resource allocation. "We fight about money and space. What else are we going to fight about?" stated one principal. This principal succinctly and accurately stated the quandary at both campuses. The limited resources coupled with the lack of transparency made it difficult for the council to negotiate and compromise. This situation made it difficult to look at the campus to assess the needs of the individual schools in the context of the collective.

Unfortunately, this is one area where the principals have received no guidance on strategies for negotiation and resolution of the issues at hand. And so every year the principals come to the table to discuss shared expenses, knowing well that one or more of the members did not meet their obligations the previous year and there was no certainty that they would do so the following year. Or they will meet to address space issues, knowing that one or more of the members will "create classes" to explain space utilization in order to justify their allotment of space without considering the current or evolving needs of the schools within it. Or worse they will continue to live with unresolved issues, knowing well that one or more members will derail the negotiation.

The creation of the Principals' Council was in recognition of building leaders' locus of control and that ultimately they were the individuals best equipped to manage a campus that was safe and orderly and conducive to teaching and learning. However, after all the jostling and fighting for space and budgets, the relationship is a strained one. And although some principals remain true to their commitment to the campus others are still struggling with the concept of autonomy and/or the collective.

The principals from both campuses agreed that their buildings were much safer than when they started. However, some of the decisions the principals made for their school came at the expense of the campus, for example, changing schedules without determining its impact on the rest of the campus or not paying their share of campus expenses. The Principals' Council, the group that should be monitoring and enforcing campus decisions, finds itself incapable of doing so. The question of legitimacy continues to play an important role in the council's impotence.

A BETTER PLAN

Creating a campus of small schools is not simply closing a large school and placing small schools in it. Closing a large school is not simply removing the students in it. The experiences of principals on these campuses underscore the complexity of the process. The process of closing a large, underperforming school and installing the small schools was chaotic. It took many years for the campus to settle down to normal school life, most of which could have potentially been reduced, if not eliminated.

The emotional stress on the school community (e.g., staff and students) was not factored into the process. The failure of central administration to take this into consideration created an enormous burden on the small-school principals as they tried to build their schools in a hostile and unwelcoming environment. A better, wiser, and more humane, and educationally sound, mechanism for closing a school is needed in order to avoid the hostility associated with the closure.

There are several options that were available and well known that would have facilitated the campus formation process (Feldman, Lopez & Simon, 2006). An option would be to incubate the small school in another location for a year and then bring them into the large building as space is carved out. Another option would be to reduce the closing-school population for a year and then allow the small schools to start up. In either option, there is sufficient time to address the concerns of the staff and students, allowing for a "humane" closing. It would also provide ample time to reduce the large-school population significantly and avoid the jostling for space.

Another issue that needs to be considered in the plan is the principals' leadership in a campus context. The assumption that several principals can share space and figure out how to manage a campus is false. This myth was unmistakably evident from the principals' conversations. The principals clearly articulated the need for someone to come in and help them negotiate and build consensus. They needed guidance from central administration. The Principals' Council requires an investment in time and resources. Central administrators need to consider the importance and the impact that a well-developed council would have in maintaining a safe and orderly environment.

Finally, principals assigned to campus schools must be able to work with other principals. The principals emphasized that the ability to work collaboratively was more important than work experience for a principal that is assigned to a campus. Campus settings are complex environments with multiple principals responsible for one building; each leader with his or her unique personality, experience, and educational commitment.

Collaborative work is a complex task. It requires consensus building among diverse and, at times, competing forces. It only takes one person for the process to come to a standstill. How to work around this person, or despite this person, is difficult. Much energy and many resources are spent on this process. There are also many missed opportunities because of it. And the more principals there are on a campus the greater the risk of not reaching consensus.

Principals who demonstrate collaborative leadership are able to negotiate the needs of their school and those of the campus. They are able to build relationships with their peers and resolve conflicts that emerge from those relationships.

I'M IMPORTANT TOO

The first few years were chaotic. The buildings were still overcrowded. Although the large schools did not receive any new freshmen class, the new small schools were receiving students. New smaller schools were occupying the building and they were taking over classrooms one by one and floor by floor. The growth of the small schools meant that the large schools had to adjust their programs to accommodate their shrinking allotment of rooms.

New traffic patterns had to be executed because students from the large schools were not allowed in the space assigned to the small schools. The small schools did not want their students to mingle with the closing-school students. Everyone was fighting for limited resources. Overcrowded hallways and disparities between the large school and the new small school created hazardous conditions conducive to jostling and fighting. It was survival of the fittest.

> There is a heedlessness about the way this is being implemented, said Leonie Haimson, the head of Class Size Matters, a parent advocacy group. No matter how many police you put in a school and no matter what kind of security procedures you put in place, there is no way to totally defuse the tension that exists in that school because of the huge amount of overcrowding and also the clear disparities between the students in the small schools as opposed to the large. (Gootman, 2004)

The staff of the phase-out school believed that the small schools were receiving preferential treatment: new furniture, new books, and new equipment. There was also the perception that the small schools were able to recruit students of higher academic caliber and left them with the bulk of Special Education students, ELL, and low-performing students, many of whom had behavioral problems.

Adding insult to injury, the small schools were seen as "skimming off the best teachers and best students" (Devine, 2004). In the minds of many, there was no reason to work so hard. The only recourse for the staff was to get new jobs, an endeavor that proved to be very difficult for many. The air was thick with anger, resentment, and hostility. And not just from the teachers. Kids were equally upset.

Students are incredibly attached to their schools, especially at the high school level. They enjoy returning to their schools after graduation and many look forward to high school reunions. Unfortunately a school that has been closed deprives its alumni from experiencing the joy of visiting their old school. Students were angry and sad. They could not understand why the school could not be fixed instead of closing.

The emotions felt by the staff and students were real. Not only was the school labeled underperforming and violent, it was being closed. The announcement was not welcomed, the decision was not theirs, and their voices were never heard. Worst still, they were viewed as the "problem" and the "reason" why the school was in such poor condition. Nevertheless someone had to be blamed and they were the perfect scapegoat.

However, the question was not whether the school should or shouldn't have closed. Everyone understood that there was a problem and that it needed to be addressed. The question should have been, "How do we address the concerns of both the large school and the new smaller school communities?" Consider how different this experience would have been if central administration had heard the voices of all the constituents.

LESSONS LEARNED

The growth of campus schools in the city has been astronomical. The city has over three hundred campuses representing over eight hundred schools at elementary and secondary levels. This number is likely to increase with co-locations of charter schools with public schools and additional school closings. Regrettably, the increase in campuses does not reflect an increase in understanding of the process of closing a school and creating a campus. And with so many schools closing simultaneously, there is little room for evaluation.

Eisner states that "no effort to change schools can succeed without designing an approach to evaluation that is consistent with the aims of the desired change" (Eisner, 1998). The lack of a mechanism to evaluate campus schools and the process of campus formation and structures generates more questions than answers.

- Are campus schools safer and more orderly because of a culture of respect, tolerance, and high expectations that has been created by the smaller learning environment or are principals less likely to report incidents?

- Is the perception of a well-managed campus the reality of a Principals' Council that has been able to balance the needs of their individual schools and that of the campus or the silence of campus conflict? Does the proliferation of campus schools reflect a viable alternative for safe and orderly environments that are more personable and conducive to teaching and learning or does it merely reflect a political agenda?
- Is the transition process effectuated in a manner that minimizes the impact of the dissolution of one school and the formation of the campus?

Without an evaluation plan, these questions and more cannot be answered empirically. Although time has given us some information, it is difficult to attribute the results—positive or negative—of the reform to any given element or aspect of the process. Not only does that make replication of the successful aspect of the reform difficult, it also allows for the duplication of mistakes.

Starting a small school requires an enormous amount of organizational planning and community relationship building and support. The stability of the school (e.g., leadership and faculty) is paramount in order to ensure its growth. On the other hand, closing a school that has been in the neighborhood for eighty or ninety years is a traumatic event for the school community, regardless of the fact that it was in poor condition.

Having these two events occurring simultaneously demonstrates little understanding of the conditions necessary for successful implementation. By understanding the elements that make up the specific qualities of the events and their interaction, an informed judgment can be made to improve a condition. Starting a new school is by no means a new concept; their start-up and development are well researched and documented.

On the other hand, campus development does not have a similar research base. That is why an evaluative dimension is needed. An evaluative dimension to any reform plan provides an opportunity for assessment. However, in order to make a value judgment on a quality (campus development), one must recognize and understand the different elements (phase-out process) that make up the specific qualities (small school start-up and school closure) and the complex interactions between them.

For school districts a clear understanding of the phase-out and start-up process will facilitate a better plan for the transition into a campus that takes into consideration both the new smaller schools and the closing school. This transitional plan would take into account not just the logistics of the process but it would also respect the emotional turmoil of the transition. Many individuals were impacted by the decision to close. By providing support and facilitating next steps for staff and students, central administration acknowledges the difficult situation and helps them move on.

In addition to district offices building their capacity and systems to support the principals on a campus, they must provide the principals training on collaborative leadership and campus management. Understanding the key elements of collaborative leadership—such as building relationships and managing the conflicts that will inevitably arise in relationships, negotiating, and reaching consensus—will assist the principals with campus management.

Equally important, for several reasons, is the need for ongoing training for the principals on a campus. First, the tenure of principals in schools has declined in the last decade. For a myriad of reasons, both the Cuomo and the Marin Campus have experienced multiple changes in leadership in the schools residing on the campus. In fact some of the small schools on the campus have experienced multiple changes within their short life span.

Each leadership change impacts the dynamics of the Principals' Council. Assuming that the transition will be smooth is false. Making assumptions about principals is where many of the problems on campuses began. A new member to any team will cause a change in dynamics. It may be a smooth transition or it may be a rocky transition, depending on the new member and his or her interaction with the other members. However, it should be the responsibility of district offices to ensure that the introduction of the new member be made respecting the dynamics of the group.

Secondly, relationships can become strained. It happens all the time, even in the corporate world. There is no reason to believe that school leaders are exempt from such situations. And unlike the corporate world, the principals on a campus cannot just dissolve the partnership. The additional training and support will help the council move past the obstacles that are preventing it from negotiating and reaching consensus. In doing so, they will be able to create a safe and orderly environment that is conducive to teaching and learning and ultimately student achievement, which was the goal of the reform.

Campus creation was the means to providing the children of NYC, regardless of where they live, with the opportunity to engage in the learning process in a personalized environment of their choice that was safe and orderly. The smaller schools evened the playing field for all children in the city to succeed academically, regardless of their socioeconomic status, gender, or race.

The campuses created during the Bloomberg/Klein administration are likely to remain, mainly due to the scale of the reform and because there is a general consensus that small school are better for learning, especially for inner-city students who have experienced more educational inequalities. Yet, if this new configuration is to be successful in maintaining a safe and orderly environment for teaching and learning to occur, then it is important to remember not to repeat the same mistakes made with the large schools. Otherwise, we will end up with campuses that are as underperforming and violent as many of the large schools that were closed.

And if a reminder is needed, let's review the introduction to this book.

References

Archer, D., & Cameron, A. (2013). Collaborative Leadership: Building Relationships, Handling Conflicts and Sharing Control. New York: Routledge.

Archibold, R. C. (1998, September 16). New Era as Police Prepare to Run School Security. www.nytimes.com/1998/09/16/nyregion/new-era-as-police-prepare-to-run-school-security.html.

Arinde, N. (2009, December 17). Activists Demand Transparency and Clarity in Proposed School Closures. http://ezalumni.library.nyu.edu:2243/printviewfile?accountid=33843.

Astor, R. A., Meyer, H. A., & Behre, W. J. (1999). Unowned Places and Times: Maps and Interviews about Violence in High Schools. *American Educational Research Journal*, 36(1), 3–42.

Baker, J. A. (1998). Are We Missing the Forest for the Trees? Considering the Social Context of School Violence. *Journal of School Psychology*, 36(1), 29–44.

Brady, K. P., Balmer, S., & Phenix, D. (2007). School-Police Partnership Effectiveness in Urban Schools: An Analysis of New York City's Impact Schools Initiative. *Education and Urban Society*, 39(4), 455–78.

Campanile, C. (2004, January 6). Dirty Dozen Schools; Mayor Names 12 Most Violent. www.nypost.com/p/news/dirty_dozen_schools_mayor_names_gyEsUN5rT1On9VPG4nYglK.html.

Clinchy, E., (2000). Creating New Schools: How Small Schools Are Changing American Education. New York: Teachers College Press.

Daniels, H., Bizar, M., & Zemelman, S., (2001). Rethinking High School: Best Practices in Teaching, Learning, and Leadership. Portsmouth, NH: Heinemann.

Devine, J. (2004). The Discourse on Violence Prevention: What Are the Implications for Smaller Schools. In J. Devine, J. Gilligan, K. A. Miczek, R. Shaikh & D. Platt (Eds), Youth Violence: Scientific Approaches to Prevention. New York: New York Academy of Sciences.

Dohrn, B. (2001). "Look Out Kid/It's Something You Did": Zero Tolerance for Children. In W. Ayers, B. Dohrn & R. Ayers (Eds.), Zero Tolerance: Resisting the Drive for Punishment in Our Schools. New York: New Press.

Donahue, E., Schiraldi, V., & Ziedenberg, J. (1998). School House Hype: School Shootings and the Real Risks Kids Face in America. Washington, DC: Justice Policy Institute.

Drum Major Institute. (2005). A Look at the Impact Schools: A Drum Major Institute Public Policy Data Brief. New York: Author

Eisner, E. W. (1998). The Enlightened Eye: Qualitative Inquiry and the Enhancement of Educational Practice. Upper Saddle River, NJ: Prentice Hall.

Elliott, D. S., Hamburg, B., & Williams, K. R. (1998). Violence in American Schools: An Overview. In D. S. Elliott, B. Hamburg & K. R. Williams (Eds.),Violence in American Schools. Cambridge, UK: Cambridge University Press.

Farrington, D. P., & Welsh, B. C. (2007). Saving Children from a Life of Crime: Early Risk Factors and Effective Communication. New York: Oxford University Press.

Feldman, J., Lopez, M. L., & Simon, K. G. (2006). Choosing Small: The Essential Guide to Successful High School Conversion. San Francisco: Jossey-Bass.

Fowler, W. J., & Walberg, H. J. (1991). School Size, Characteristics, and Outcomes. *Educational Evaluation and Policy Analysis*, 13(2), 189–202.

Garbarino, J. (1978). The Human Ecology of School Crime: A Case for Small Schools. In E. Wenk and N. Harlow (Eds.), School Crime and Disruption (155–64). Davis, CA: Responsible Action.

Garcia, C. A. (2003). School Safety Technology in America: Current Use and Perceived Effectiveness. *Criminal Justice Policy Review*, 14(1), 30–54.

Gootman, E. (2004a, January 6). Police to Guard 12 City Schools Cited as Violent. www.nytimes.com/2004/01/06/nyregion/police-to-guard-12-city-schools-cited-as-violent.html.

Gootman, E. (2004b, March 25). Crime Falls as Citations Surge in Schools with Extra Officers. www.nytimes.com/2004/03/25/nyregion/crime-falls-as-citations-surge-in-schools-with-extra-officers.html.

Gootman, E. (2004c, April 16). 4 High Schools Added to Those That Require Extra Security. www.nytimes.com/2004/04/16/nyregion/4-high-schools-added-to-those-that-require-extra-security.html.

Gootman, E. (2004d, December 15). More Police, but Halls Are Still Jammed at Unruly School. www.nytimes.com/2004/12/15/nyregion/ 15walton.html.

Gordon, R., Della Piana, L., & Kelcher, T. (2001). Zero Tolerance: A Basic Report Card. In W. Ayers, B. Dohrn & R. Ayers (Eds.), Zero Tolerance: Resisting the Drive for Punishment in Our Schools. New York: New Press.

Gorman-Smith, D. (2003). The Social Ecology of Community and Neighborhood and Risk for Antisocial Behavior. In C. A. Essau (Ed.), Conduct and Oppositional Defiant Disorders: Epidemiology, Risk Factors, and Treatment. Mahwah, NJ: Lawrence Erlbaum.

Gottfredson, D. C. (2001). Schools and Delinquency. Cambridge, UK: Cambridge University Press.

Gottfredson, G. D., & Gottfredson, D. C. (1985). Victimization in Schools. New York: Plenum Press.

Gumpel, T. P. (2008). Behavioral Disorder in the School: Participants Roles and Sub-Roles in Three Types of School Violence. *Journal of Emotional and Behavioral Disorders*, 16(3), 145–62.

Hannington, D. (2013, April 3). Parents, Teachers, and Students Rally against School Closings. http://ezalumni.library.nyu.edu:2243/printviewfile?accountid= 33843.

Herszenhorn, D. M. (2005, June 23). Crime Is Down in 6 Schools on City's Most-Troubled List. www.nytimes.com/2005/06/23/ nyregion/23impact.html.

Holloway, L. (1998, September 17). Board Votes to Give Police Control over School Security. www.nytimes.com/1998/09/17/nyregion/board-votes-to-give-police-control-over-school-security.html.

Lane, K. L., Carter, E. W., Pierson, M. R., & Glasser, B. C. (2006). Academic, Social, and Behavioral Characteristics of High School Students with Emotional Disturbances or Learning Disabilities. *Journal of Emotional and Behavioral Disorders*, 14(2), 108–17.

Lee, V. E., & Burkam, D. T. (2003). Dropping out of High School: The Role of School Organization and Structure. *American Educational Research Journal*, 40(2), 353–93.

Lee, V. E., & Ready, D. D. (2007). Schools within Schools: Possibilities and Pitfalls of High School Reform. New York: Teachers College Press.

Lee, V. E., Smerdon, B. A., Alfeld-Liro, C., & Brown, S. L. (2000). Inside Large and Small High Schools: Curriculum and Social Relations. *Educational Evaluation and Policy Analysis*, 22(2), 147–71.

Lee, V. E., & Smith, J. B. (1995). Effects of High School Restructuring and Size on Early Gains in Achievement and Engagement. *Sociology of Education*, 68(40), 241–70.

Lee, V. E., & Smith, J. B. (1997). High School Size: Which Works Best and for Whom? *Educational Evaluation and Policy Analysis*, 19(3), 205–27.

Meir, D. (1996). The Power of Their Ideas: Lessons for America from a Small School in Harlem. Boston: Beacon Press.

Menacker, J., Weldon, W., & Hurwitz, E. (1990). Community Influences on School Crime and Violence. *Urban Education*, 25(1), 68–80.

Moore, M. (1988). What Sort of Ideas Become Public Ideas? In R. B. Reich (Ed.), The Power of Public Ideas. Cambridge, MA: Harvard University Press.

New York City Department of Education. (2003). Mayor Michael R. Bloomberg and Schools Chancellor Joel I. Klein Announce New School Safety Plan. Retrieved July 5, 2008, from http://schools.nyc.gov/Offices/ mediarelations/NewsandSpeeches/2003-2004/12-23-2003-13-2-36- 874.htm.

Noguera, P. A. (1995). Preventing and Producing Violence: A Critical Analysis of Responses to School Violence. *Harvard Educational Review*, 65(2), 189–207.

Noguera, P. A. (2000). Listen First: How Student Perspectives on Violence Can Be Used to Create Safer Schools. In V. Polakow (Ed.), The Public Assault on America's Children. New York: Teachers College Press.

Noguera, P. A. (2001). Finding Safety Where We Least Expect It: The Role of Social Capital in Preventing School Violence. In W. Ayers, B. Dohrn & R. Ayers (Eds.), Zero Tolerance: Resisting the Drive for Punishment in Our Schools. New York: New Press.

Nolan, K. (2011). Police in the Hallways: Discipline in an Urban High School. Minneapolis: University of Minnesota Press.

Osterman, K. (2000). Students' Need for Belonging in the School Community. *Review of Educational Research*, 70(3), 323–67.

Otterman, S., & Medina, J. (2010, January 27). Boos and Personal Attacks as City Panel Prepares to Vote on School Closings. http://ezalumni.library.nyu.edu:2243/printview?accountid=33843.

Patterson, G. R., DeBaryshe, B. D., & Ramsey, E. (1989). A Developmental Perspective on Antisocial Behavior. *American Psychologist*, 44, 329–35.

Peterson, R., & Skiba, R. (2000). Creating School Climates That Prevent School Violence. *Preventing School Failure*, Spring 2000, 122–29.

Polakow-Suransky, S. (1999). America's Least Wanted: Zero Tolerance Policies and the Fate of Expelled Students. In V. Polakow (Ed.), The Public Assault on America's Children: Poverty, Violence, and Juvenile Injustice. New York: Teachers College Press.

Roberts, S., Ahang, J., & Truman, J. (2012). Indicators of School Crime and Safety: 2011 (NCES 2012-002/NCJ 236021). National Center for Education Statistics, Institute of Education Sciences, U.S. Department of Education, and Bureau of Justice Statistics, Office of Justice Programs, U.S. Department of Justice, Washington, D.C.

Sampson, R. J. (2001). How Do Communities Undergird or Undermine Human Development? Relevant Contexts and Social Mechanisms. In A. Booth & A. C. Crouter (Eds.), Does It Take a Village? Community Effects on Children, Adolescents, and Families. Mahwah, NJ: Lawrence Erlbaum.

Saulny, S. (2004, October 19). City Adapts a Police Strategy to Violent Schools. www.nytimes.com/2004/10/19nyregion/19safety.html.

Saulney, S. (2005, January 4). City Cites Gains in Combating School Violence. www.nytimes.com/2005/01/04/nyregion/04school.html.

Saulney, S. (2005, August 3). Noncrime Disturbances Rise at Tough Schools. www.nytimes.com/2005/08/03/nyregion/03safety.html.

Schwartz, R., & Rieser, L. (2001). Zero Tolerance as Mandatory Sentencing. In W. Ayers, B. Dohrn & R. Ayers (Eds.), Zero Tolerance: Resisting the Drive for Punishment in Our Schools. New York: New Press.

Scott, W. R. (2001). Institutions and Organizations. Thousand Oaks, CA: Sage.

Siskin, L. S. (2011). Changing Contexts and the Challenge of High School Reform in New York City. In J. A. O'Day, C. S. Bitter & L. H. Gomez (Eds.), Education Reform in New York City. Cambridge, MA: Harvard Education Press.

Skiba, R. J., & Peterson, R. L. (1999). The Dark Side of Zero Tolerance: Can Punishment Lead to Safe Schools? *Phi Delta Kappan*, 80, 372–82.

Small, S., & Supple, A. (2001). Communities as Systems: Is a Community More Than the Sum of Its Parts? In A. Booth & A. C. Crouter (Eds.), Does It Take a Village? Community Effects on Children, Adolescents, and Families. Mahwah, NJ: Lawrence Erlbaum.

Sprague, J., Walker, H. M., Stieber, S., Simonsen, B., Nishioka, V., & Wagner, L. (2001). Exploring the Relationship between School Discipline Referrals and Delinquency. *Psychology in the Schools*, 38(2), 197–206.

Toch, T. (2003). *High Schools on a Human Scale: How Small Schools Can Transform American Education*. Boston: Beacon Press.

Wagner, M., Kutash, K., Duchnowski, A. J., Epstein, M. H., & Sumi, W. C. (2005). The Children and Youth We Serve: A National Picture of the Characteristics of Students with Emotional Disturbances Receiving Special Education. *Journal of Emotional and Behavioral Disorders*, 13(2), 79–96.

Walker, H. M., Gresham, F. M., & Ramsey, E. (2004). *Antisocial Behavior in School: Evidence-Based Practices*. Belmont, CA: Wadsworth/Thompson Learning.

Welsh, W. N. (2000). The Effects of School Crime on School Disorder. *Annals of the American Academy of Political and Social Science*, 567, 88–107.

About the Author

Mónica Ortiz has served the children of New York City for 22 years after working in the accounting field for 10 years. She has worked for the NYC Department of Education in various capacities. As teacher, Mónica taught at the middle school and high school levels. She was an Assistant Principal for Administration. She served as Director of Student Suspension for the city. As a Principal for 11 years, Mónica has been successful in turning around challenging schools in NYC with an unwavering belief in students' ability to succeed. Mónica earned a B.S in Accounting and a M.S. in Education from Lehman College. She received her C.A.S in Educational Administration and earned an ED.D in Educational Administration from New York University.

www.ingramcontent.com/pod-product-compliance
Lightning Source LLC
Chambersburg PA
CBHW030145240426
43672CB00005B/276